HOW TO MAKE
LIFE EASIER:

THE COMPLETE GUIDE
ON HOW TO DECLUTTER,
DE-STRESS, CLEAN AND
ORGANISE YOUR HOME

Darlene Tucker

Table of content

Introduction

Have you noticed that this society emphasizes success by how much you have rather than happiness? I have found that I hate the fact that my success is based on how much I have. Sure, it might be nice to have the new gadgets and everything you could want, but in the end, is it worth it? No possession or amount of activity can satisfy your need for success. Success is defined differently for different people. Sure, some might thrive off of having more and more. However, our human nature isn't dependent upon having access. We have simple needs that we need to be met, but beyond that, everything has just considered a luxury. When we make our luxuries into needs, then we tend to be unhappy.

I'm not stressed out with trying to obtain more and what I have is sufficient. When I finally came to that mindset, it was a huge relief. I didn't feel like I needed to do everything to accomplish a goal that wasn't even necessary.

How about you? Do you find that you're stressed out by thinking about all you have to do to maintain what you have? Take a close look at your life. Do you have access that you're trying to keep? Are there things that you consider to be an essential need but do not need? If your answer to any of these questions is"yes," I encourage you to read this book and reevaluate what is a need as opposed to what is a luxury. What you might find out about yourself might surprise you.

If you're looking to simplify your life, I encourage you to continue reading. In this book, I'm going to give you some hints and tips on how to declutter, de-stress, clean and organize your home so that you can enjoy what you have. You might find that the simple life is the way to go and love it as much as I do!

Principle 1: What do you need for effective cleaning and organization?

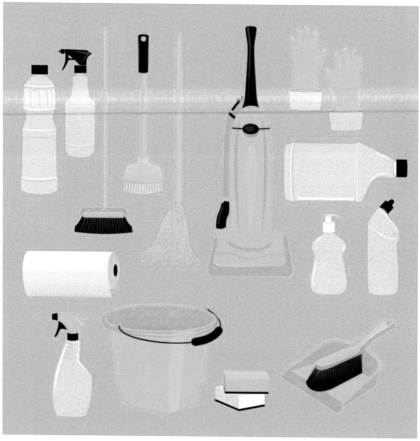

Vacuum Steam Cleaner

A productive steam cleaner can manage the hardest grime and soil and is extraordinary compared to other cleaning machines accessible for hard surface cleaning. The cleaning power comes fundamentally from the yield temperature of the PC, which can reach up to 386°F.

A few models are using the most recent innovations accessible available. Nonetheless, it is critical to utilize machines that can complete an assortment of cleaning capacities easily and in the briefest conceivable time. Yield temperature is maybe the most basic thought when looking for a steam clothes washer. The higher the temperature, the more proficient machines are as they are regularly spotless. High temperatures enable gadgets to break down soil and recolor, and unstick concealed polluting influences from difficult to places.

A dry vapor steam cleaner is a propelled cleaning gadget that makes a portion of the hardest cleaning errands generally straightforward. Steam clothes washers join warmth and strain to diminish and overwhelm stains; making it easier to wipe away the remaining stores. Dry vapor steam is particularly valuable for cleaning business fridges. You can utilize the machines to clean profound coolers in light of the fact that the steam frameworks unstick layered stores effortlessly without harming coolers and refrigerators.

The most recent innovation would now be able to dispense with more than 99 percent of germs and microbes from any hard surface. The vapor steam encourages simple evacuation of fluid waste with an incorporated vacuum and a large group of different apparatuses for more deep cleaning and simple access to bigger territories. The dry steam yield is a condition of superheated water where the dampness content is under five percent. Vapor steam cleaning machines are generally utilized as a part of the social insurance and friendliness enterprises as they clean and, with the correct advancements, disinfect the surface. Where sterile cleaning is a need, a vapor steam clothes washer is the machine that can do the assignment thoroughly and rapidly. A propelled steam vacuum cleaner conveys unmatched cleaning comes about and guarantees speedier cleaning. The gadgets offer a preferred critical standpoint with regards to business cleaning in spots, for example, eateries and kitchens. In the event that you are hoping to clean local locations with a steam vacuum cleaner, at that point the best cleaning hardware for such circumstances is the compact steam clothes washer.

A versatile steam cleaner utilizes little water for cleaning, depending more on the energy of steam to clean extreme stains and grime. They are likewise powerful as floor steam clothes washers in healing facilities and centers to keep the place shining clean and sans germ. Steam cleaner machines offer the advantage of utilizing little water amid the cleaning procedure, making them perfect for indoor cleaning.

Continuously pick floor steam cleaners from reputable organizations to ensure you get your coveted cleaning targets finished. The best steam clothes washers can convey extraordinary cleaning comes about on the hardest cleaning surfaces.

Tools for organizing space

Regardless of whether you live in an apartment or a vast house, there dependably is by all accounts no less than one space that is not arranged to fit your needs. The things you need to store won't fit where you require them to go. Pantry, storage room, or kitchen- - you will discover a sorting out test someplace in your home. There are approaches to overcome space.

Frequently storerooms are just fitted with a rack and a hanging bar. The setup is fine if the totals of what you have are long hanging garments. If not, consider introducing racks - either appended to the divider or an unsupported unit- - in one area of the wardrobe. Racks hold a great deal of collapsed garments, containers of clothing, toiletries, even your flood of books.

Make utilization of snares. They hold everything from keys to coats. They can likewise be enriching. Utilize snares with a releasable cement backing for places where you can't penetrate gaps. They arrive in an assortment of weight confines and are effectively evacuated without damaging dividers or entryways.

The ever-prevalent clear plastic canisters are priceless arranging devices in little spaces. Mark them with their substance and tuck them up on high retires or under the bed- - an incredible stockpiling answer for regular things. Utilize clear receptacles as sliding drawers in vanity cupboards, cloth storerooms, or under the kitchen sink. Ensure you assemble like things. Measure the stature, profundity, and width of your stockpiling regions so you can buy the best possible size receptacles.

Utilize vertical space. A divider unit with racks and cupboards can hold beautifying things and books. They likewise can be loaded with wicker bin, canvas receptacles, and other alluring compartments to compose things which rapidly mess a little space- - office supplies, little PC parts, camera gear, magazines, make supplies, memorabilia. Once more, name the substance.

In the clothing region, utilize snare racks or individual snares to hold floor brushes, mops, and dusters. Utilize racks and cupboards for cleaning supplies. On the off chance that the washer and dryer fill the entire space, consider utilizing a detached bureau to store cleanser and other cleaning supplies in a contiguous lobby or room.

No space to store gems? Hang a little release board and utilize stick pins to hold pieces of jewelry and armlets flawlessly. Similarly, utilize a pivoted shadowbox. This stockpiling arrangement does twofold obligation as a craftsmanship piece.

In any case, you will free up floor space by putting away shoes all the more productively in a composed way.

Purchase amounts which fit your storage room. On the off chance that you have constrained pantry stockpiling, take a pass on the discount store measure cleanser. The same applies to the 30-move pack of latrine tissue in a one-room condo.

Before you buy, inquire as to whether the thing has a space in your home. What's more, inquire as to whether the thing will be messiness. Be straightforward, regardless of the possibility that you need to leave behind the One Day Only Extra 15% off deal. Consider the esteem versus the exacerbation - spare a dollar or have a messiness free home you appreciate.

How to use the timer?

Much is said in regards to time administration. In any case, the term has started to apply to a wide assortment of subjects running from list administration, venture administration and even up to keeping up one's vitality. All these are critical; however we have to take a gander at the term itself., If one takes a gander at the words 'time administration, 'you will realize that they are referring to the management of time. It incorporates the administration of the seconds, minutes and the hours of our day.

I have discovered, maintaining a few organizations and wearing many caps (as do a considerable lot of us) that the utilization of a basic commencement clock can work wonders. I need to call attention to seven reasons why utilizing a clock can enable us to accomplish progressively and even lessen stretch.

Here are seven great reasons why every one of us ought to utilize a commencement clock:

1) Timers enhance our familiarity with time. A first administer of effectively dealing with anything is to go up against and end up noticeably mindful of it. Similarly, as we get overweight in life by sitting out of gear eating and not focusing on what we put in our mouths, we can likewise squander our valuable time as if it is a boundless ownership. The main reason why weight control plans work is that they make us focus on what we are eating. Our utilization of calories, of cash, and of our chance extends past what we require and what is solid unless we wind up noticeably mindful of how we utilize these items. We should know about these things to control them. Utilization of a clock is the best approach to get mindful of and to oversee time.

2) Timers break time into reasonable bits. Objectives are best

vanquished in stages, in degrees, and steps. The hours in our day are no exemptions. Clocks enable us to break our lives and exercises into sensible bits.

3) Just as an eating routine contains a solid choice not to surpass your caloric admission or fall short of our settled upon work out., a commencement clock, alongside an individual consent to play by the guidelines, will help shield us from straying starting with one errand then onto the next. Fruitful multitasking is a myth. We finish the most by doing things each one in turn. The choice to utilize and to take after the commencement clock encourages us to stay with our own decisions and causes us to keep up the train in our utilization of time.

4) Timers cause shows us to take a gander at assignments with respect to units of time. Instead of simply say "I'm going shopping" one takes a gander at the activity as an hour and a half duty, and this predicts exactly how it fits into the hours we have amid the day. This forces a kind of request on our opportunity and our lives. This can unquestionably decrease push.

5) Timers help a spot dawdled and, actually, help us to assess if that time is genuinely squandered or not. For example, on the off chance that we causatively put aside a limited period for intrusions and a clock, appropriately utilized, can enable us to control those interferences. It is something like keeping a journal of what we eat and the intermittent stun concerning the amount we set away you're waking hours. Utilizing a clock enables us to designate better where we invest our energy.

6) Using a clock makes it conceivable to comprehend the idea of the activity. All errands, all activities that we do or take amid the day are cycles of activity. A time of work dependably has a beginning, change, and a stop. This comprehension can force a mind-blowing measure of rational soundness into how we work in our lives. A clock is an incredible method for accentuating this key truth of life.

7) There's nothing amiss with loafing. A commencement clock can put great control into our falsehoods enabling us to discover time to move, to play, to sleep and to do all things that are virtuous. Once more, with the eating regimen similitude, we adore our pastries once in a while yet we should be mindful so as not to escape with them. This is similar to stacking time. A commencement clock causes us to guarantee that we have sufficient energy to play and encourages us to keep a component of control over those minutes, so they are legitimately adjusted with the other vital things in life.

Despite the fact that a clock, utilized effectively, will go far to enhance the nature of our lives, the expansion of a smidgen of day by day arranging alongside the usage of a clock will duplicate the value of that clock no less than ten times.

Things Required to Clean Your House

There are certain cleaning items which every house needs to have so that the house stays sparkling clean. It is also advisable to restock your cleaning items in bulk so that you do not keep rushing out to buy smaller portions of these items. Here are some of the basic tools you can use to keep dirt away from the house without necessarily going out to get some of the missing cleaning items.

You should maintain cleanliness in your house at all times because you have to live and rest there. It should be stainless and should smell the best when you enter the house. If you do not clean the house, then the dust can sit on things making it look bad and can cause you to suffer from disease. Cleanliness is critical because the more an environment is clean, the better it is for you and your family.

Mostly it is the woman who takes the responsibility to clean the house; so she knows best when to restock the cleaning stuff for the house.

No one likes to keep the house messy which is why when you are enthusiastic to clean the house, make sure you have the right items. There are a lot of them so here is the list of some which you need to have to do the cleaning at home.

To kill the germs:

- Baking soda

- White vinegar

- Rubbing alcohol

- Lemons

- Hand-wash dishwasher detergent

- Laundry detergent

- Dishwasher liquid detergent

- Chlorine bleach

- Fabric softener

- Fabric Bleach

- Bathroom cleaners

- Carpet stain remover

- Glass cleaner

- Stainless steel cleaner

- Oven cleaner

- For Furniture:

- Wood furniture cleaner

- Leather furniture cleaner

- Brass fix

- For the house overall:

- Soft rags

- Dustpan

- Vacuum Cleaner

- Bucket

- Paper towels

- Sponges

- Mops

- Scrubbers

These are some of the things which you are required to have in order to make your work easier when cleaning the house.

Cleaning and Organizing Supplies

It is about time that we gave some thought to the ingredients required to do all this work, their storage, and maintenance. As you would have already seen in the previous chapters, most of the materials used are stuff that can be locally sourced without much ado. These cleaning materials are not only plentiful but also safe as they are not necessarily toxic.

By now all of you would have come to terms with the fact that it is indeed possible to maintain a world-class home without shelling out a fortune on cleaning supplies and cleaning crews. I hope this book has managed to deprive your mind off the misconception that stacks of cleaning supplies in departmental stores are the only answer to maintaining a clean and hygienic household.

As of now, I believe I have managed to inculcate a basic idea of how to use the stuff lying around in your home in a very safe and efficient manner. Some research into the products available in the market can make it very clear that the cleaning chemicals are not as safe as they claim to be. They contain a lot of hazardous chemicals which usually prove to be very harmful when used with such proximity and frequency. The safety standards that you can achieve with the use of standard household items cannot be stressed enough.

The same analogy applies to organizing your stuff. Many of the things that we use in our daily lives can be recycled and put to better use. There are many ways that you can become resourceful and creative without having to worry about an interior designer cleaning your wallet out. Let us see what kind of resources you will have to stock to make good use of all the techniques that were discussed in this book.

- Lemons are a readily available resource, and they can be exploited to a considerable extent. They are composed of citric acid, which although capable of removing stains is not strong enough by itself . Thanks to the bleaching property of lemons, they can be used in combination with a lot of products. An added advantage is that the fruits can be used to provide a fresh and long lasting smell as well.

- Essential oils are available in an extensive variety. Although their cleaning properties do not amount to much, they can be used to make your space more hospitable. Their primary job is to provide much-needed fragrance to the surroundings. Given the wide assortment that is available today, this task is nothing great for them.

- Microfiber cloth is a must have for every household. It is an integral part of any do-it-yourself cleaning kit. This cloth is made with strands that are significantly smaller than a strand of silk. Due to their excellent texture, these clothes are used to wipe or polish very delicate surfaces without harming the surface. They can be ideal for cleaning susceptible surfaces like LCDs and monitors. With microfiber cloths, you can be sure the cleaning job will be excellent without compromising on the quality of the finish of the product. Their molecules are electrically unbalanced; for this reason, they tend to stick to all kinds of surfaces, including dirt.

- Rags are a lifesaver and a must have in most cleaning scenarios. They are especially useful when cleaning a particularly smelly mess. Rags are expendable and can be thrown away after use without a second thought. They are also readily available and can be sourced without much ado. They have multiple uses, and one among them is their ability to soak up a significant amount of fluid mess. They can be used to make a big mess reduce in size so that we can focus on finer cleaning. They are completely capable of handling all the first cleaning by themselves.

- Sponges are a necessity at times where we require an absorbent as nothing absorbs better than a sponge. They can absorb and clean to some extent without damaging or scratching the surface that they are supposed to clean. Sponges are also cheap and easily available. They are most commonly used to clean delicate surfaces with water or other solvents. They could be perfect for glass, car bodies, *etc.*

- Mops have been making cleaning an easy task since their invention. It ensures that we do not have to go through a lot of physical strain while cleaning floors. Usually, we would find ourselves on our hands and knees with a pail of water and a rag to clean the floors. It would also require some effort on our part to clean under the furniture and in those hard to reach corners. A mop takes away more than half of these worries. We do not have to bend or exert that much of a physical strain while using a mop for cleaning. The long handles of the mop allow us to be comfortable standing while cleaning up the floor. It also makes it possible to clean under the furniture and in the corners without having to move around a large amount of stuff. Mops are completely reusable, unlike rags. They can be used to clean one mess, and they can be cleaned before cleaning another kind of a mess.

- Newspapers are perhaps the cheapest and most effective collateral that you can find in your homemade cleaning kit. Papers become obsolete after a few days of printing unless we require it to refer something in the past. In most cases, newspapers become practically useless after a few days. One of the best ways to reuse old newspapers is to use them as disposable cleaning rags. They can be thrown away safely after use as they degrade very quickly.

- Castile soap is a vegetable-based soap that is made using olive oil. This kind of soap is completely natural and does not employ the use of chemicals as seen in the manufacture of other soaps. It means that Castile soaps are completely biodegradable and do not have any side effect. This also makes them eligible for use in a variety of ways like mopping the floor, scrub, *etc.*

- Dishwashing liquid is beautiful for diluting stronger cleaning solutions, or they can be used in a mixture of other day to day combinations. Although dishwashing liquid is a cleaning agent, it is not as high as usual cleaning agents. They can also be strengthened by adding other daily substances. Their chemical nature allows them to be mixed with almost any kind of combination.

- Cornstarch is another item that is a definite requirement in a do-it-yourself cleaning kit. Primarily used as a constituent in baking, its capabilities extend way beyond that. It can also be used to clean a lot of everyday household items. It is particularly useful in removing carpet stains.

- Baking soda is mostly left overnight on stains as a paste and then washed off in the morning.

- Vinegar is similar to lemons and dishwashing liquids because it can use in combination with a lot of stuff without compromising on the quality of cleaning. It is primarily used to mop up after stains.

- Old toothbrushes are handier than you realize. They can clean in those crevices where your hands might not reach. The number of bristles on the toothbrush also ensures that cleaning is done properly.

- Q tips can be used for complete cleaning in those tiny holes where dirt seems to accumulate. They can be dipped in rubbing alcohol or vinegar and used to clean stains off bedspreads, carpets, *etc.*

- Rags can be soaked in vodka and used to clean ceramic and metallic surfaces.

- Steel wool is a tough core cleaning equipment. They are not soft or gentle, and so they cannot be employed in those areas where delicate work is required. There might be stains that are too concentrated to be removed by vinegar or rubbing alcohol. In such cases, steel wool can be used to eliminate a large part of the stain by scrubbing. The remaining layer can be easily removed using a natural stain removing agent.

- Hooks are a piece of equipment that would be worth investing in. They can be employed to hang up things that you require very frequently. For example, it might be easier to hang up your coat rather than fold it every day.

- Magnets are capable of saving a lot of time. There might have been instances where you would have spent hours picking up after a spilled mess in the form of paper clips or nails. A magnet would have been such a lifesaver in those situations. Magnets can also be used for storing such small metallic items.

- Labeling everything saves a lot of time and effort, so it would be wise to invest in a labeler.

- Hydrogen peroxide is an excellent cleaning agent, and they can be used in a variety of ways. It is mostly used to clean floors and walls.

Spray bottles provide the much-needed moisture and lubrication necessary for a surface to be cleaned. This enables the microfiber cloth or sponge to be utilized to its maximum potential.

Tips to Keep Your House Always Clean

Cleaning the house is nothing more than developing the habit to clean it in your regular activities. Just like you wake up and have breakfast, but if you clean your house before that, it will be better. The more you do it, the better you get at it. Do not consider it as a burden on you because it affects you psychologically and you are not able to do anything. You can get together with your spouse and develop the habits to clean the house daily with few tips here. Keeping the house clean all the time never hurts, and it does not even consume time when you have someone to do with you. It takes half of the time when you clean the house if your spouse or children help you.

1. Clean the bed

When you wake up in the morning, the first thing which you need to do is to make your bed. Make sure you spread the sheet, and there is no lump on it. Tighten it from all sides and fold the blankets. Put the pillows in the right place and make the bed perfect. It will not even take a minute, and you will be in a habit to do it every day.

2. Kitchen Counters

Keep the counters clean and tidy all the time. Do not keep the unwashed dishes on it or leave them just like that with having food in it. Make sure there is nothing on the counters when you are about to sleep. Put everything away or wash them lightly and turn on the dishwasher before sleeping. It is automated so when it will be done then it will turn off by itself. So keep a check on that and keep the kitchen clean for sure.

3. Get Timers

If you think that cleaning takes time and you will not be able to get to your office on time, then consider to set a timer today and see how long it takes. You will find that it takes lesser time than you think. In case you feel as though cleaning everything at once is difficult, you will only need to change your mindset as it is not hard; you can easily get it all done in the shortest time possible. Set the timer on your phone and then check it when you are done. Or you can configure the alarm for one hour and see what you get done before the bell rings or not. Keep the usual speed of cleaning, and you will be out of the doubt for sure.

4. Get started with Small first

Begin with the areas that are less messy. For instance, if you find that your room is clean and you just need to do the dusting today then do that first. Move to other places and check whether they need some cleaning today. For example, if a room is too messy then you do need to fix that but later. Rate it according to the messiness which every room has. Consider to walk around the house and then keep on doing the fixtures all along. Do not keep postponing the cleaning because then it will never be cleaned.

5. Create Schedule

Make sure you act upon the calendar because it is an important task to do. Do not choose to have lazy days over the weekend and keep on missing for the cleaning part; instead, follow your schedule to the letter.

6. Assign a Basket

This is an excellent way to maintain the cleanliness of the room. Keep a basket in every room where all stuff which is not in its place can be placed. Such as if you have clothes on the sofa and you do not feel like hanging them then consider to put it in the basket for the time being and when you get the time then hang it inside. This way your room will not look messy and nothing will get lost as you can look into all that at your own convenience.

7. Clean the Easy Way

Get the right materials to clean the house more easily. If you have the right sprays and the sweepers, then you can clean the house in no time. If you use your supplies, then it will surely take the time to clean the grease from the sink. So be wise and choose the easy way by getting the right supplies for particular cleaning area.

Principle 2: Getting rid of unnecessary things

Avoid impulse buying

Avoid, wherever you can, the temptation to spend on impulse. If you always give yourself a "cooling off period," you'll minimize emotional spending or buy something just because of sneaky advertising. For smaller purchases, wait 24 hours, and for bigger purchases, sleep on it for a few days before committing.

When you're spending money on something, don't focus only on the price you see in front of you. Ask yourself what this item *costs you*.

How long did you have to work to afford it? By working that long and exchanging that time for money for this article, did you get a "real deal"? Could you use that time or that money on something else, that's worth more to you? Is that money worth more *unspent*, *i.e.,* do you have to buy anything at all?

Fast forward purchases a few years. Many of us throw away massive amounts of junk from our homes every year and also keep buying things obsessively, never making the connection between the two. Are you going to get bored of this item within a few months? Will it last? How will it fit into your life? Are you just buying next year's junk?

Don't go to shopping malls unless you're feeling calm, rational and in control. This means avoiding the shops when you're hungry, sad, bored, angry. You'll only be extra susceptible to advertising and pressure to "buy solutions." You'll have to work extra hard to resist temptation and may fall into the trap of feeling that you're depriving yourself.

Be prepared. It's so much easier to act wisely when you're acting according to a plan you've spent time on beforehand. Know how much you can afford to spend on a night out before you leave. Go shopping with a list and don't buy anything, not on that list. Pack a work lunch the night before so you're not tempted to buy something expensive on the spur of the moment when you get hungry.

Try to see if you can spend your money on lived experiences rather than things. Things get old. They break. People get bored of them. But happy memories can last a lifetime, and if your experience teaches you a new skill or gives you a fresh insight on life, even better.

Carry only small amounts of cash on you, for emergencies. It will deter you from spending mindlessly. It's easy to think of a few coins in your wallet as nothing much, but they add up. Spending on bank cards has the added advantage of letting you track exactly how much and on what you spend your money.

If you're trying to develop your professional career, you might like to consider negotiating for and working towards a higher hourly rate with less total time worked rather than endlessly angling for more work. In the long term, you'll value your *time* more and more. As you up skill and become more experienced, look for more job flexibility, more benefits and more free time rather than just a higher salary. Employers are usually a bit happier to negotiate on these anyway, and they'll have a greater impact on your quality of life.

When making big spending decisions, consider how a choice will mature with time. It may be that it's better to spend on X rather than Y in the present moment, but wait ten years, and X just gets worse and worse as a choice. When considering big purchases, spending on education or paying off debt, ask yourself what will give you the greatest flexibility and control in the future. Ask which choice gives you more options later on. Give less weight to decisions that can't be undone or modified and more weight to those that can.

Don't be afraid to talk about money. Let go of hang-ups and ask for help and advice when you need it. There's no shame in having money difficulties or being stuck with debt – but it's a real shame if you let hang-ups about money prevent you from tackling a serious problem head-on.

Some of our most nonsensical spending habits are closely tied with our worst life habits in general. Do you have an unhealthy drinking or smoking habit? It is the kind of thing you pay for over and over again – you pay for the substance itself, you pay with diminished health, and you may even have to pay later on for medicine or treatment for health problems you bring on yourself. When it comes to any addiction, it's never worth it. If this is you, the best thing you can do for yourself is clean up this bad habit. Drop your nasty sugar addiction. Quit smoking. Cut back on drinking. Vow to stay away from junk food.

Speaking of habits, there's one that you can get rid of instantly: gambling. If you're throwing away money on casinos or lottery tickets (or, as my grandmother called it, "idiot tax") then just stop. That money will do far more for you as savings.

Avoid comparing yourself to others. There's a lot of egos bound up in money, and it's hard to break the automatic connection that money = success. If you're suffering from trying to keep up with your peers, try to remember that people willfully display the life they want you to see, and there are invariably problems that you never know about. Keep going towards your own goals. If someone's success feels intimidating, try to turn that feeling into inspiration – how can you do the same? What can you learn from them?

How to Reduce Your Belongings

As highlighted in the previous chapter, our belongings tend to be the number one thing that keeps us from having a dull life. Even though they are just stuff, we tend to form emotional bonds with those things that can be difficult to break. However, it might be necessary to break this bond if you're looking to simplify your life. This can take some time and patience on your part. No one wants to admit that something that they like is nothing more than a thing. So, I'm going to give you some tips and hints on how to reduce your belongings to live a happier life.

Go Through Everything You Own

Depending on how much you own, this can be quite the undertaking. However, it will be necessary to downsize your belongings to a manageable level. The first thing that I recommend is that you go through every item you own. Take a close look at them, and separate them into piles. Have a stack for what you will for sure keep, one for the maybes, and one to get rid of. Do this room by room so that your house won't look like a total and complete wreck. The items that you can safely say that you need to can be put back right away, and you can evaluate the rest of it later on.

Evaluate whether what you have before you are needed

This is a test of your will. Take some time and look at your stuff. Ask yourself whether or not you need the item and whether or not you will ever use the thing on a regular basis. Imagine how your life would be without it. If you can safely say that you don't need it, get rid of it. Its better, to be honest with yourself and do it all at once than finding out later that you kept something around that resulted in clutter.

Donate or Sell Your Excess Stuff

This is another necessary part of your puzzle. Now is the time to get rid of the items that you have decided that you don't need. I prefer to donate them to a thrift store or have a garage sale. For some, donating it is the easiest option. For me, I enjoy having a yearly garage sale and getting rid of things. Not only does it make me money, but I also have the chance to invite friends or family to bring their stuff, and it's like a reunion. However, arranging a garage sale can be time-consuming and stressful if you don't go about it in the right way.

Have Someone Help You

Some people refuse to seek help. However, if you're living with others, they need to be on the same page as you, so enlisting their help will be necessary. Even if you live alone, having a friend come over and help you to get rid of some unnecessary stuff can both be fun and helpful. You never know, your friend might just take some of that stuff off of your hands for you and that's one less worry later on!

Asking for help is not a sign of weakness. It's only saying that you want to make a change and that you want another person to be a part of that change. So, don't worry about someone thinking you're weak for asking for help. You're just trying to do what is best for you.

Give it to Family or Friends

Having younger (or older) siblings can be another fun way to get rid of your unwanted belongings. For me, I have a sister who loves my taste in clothing and home décor, so when I asked if she wanted to come over and take some of the items I was getting rid of, she was excited. You might have a friend who is like that for you. Knowing someone who shares your tastes is a good way to recycle some of the old stuff you intend to get rid of. If you have some family or friends, who would love to relieve you of your excess belongings, don't be afraid to ask them! It could benefit both of you.

Be Heartless

This is one tip that has helped me along the way. Since I base a lot of emotional value on some of my belongings, when I go to get rid of them, I find that I doubt my decision based upon that bond. It could be something that I got with my mother that brings back memories. However, this is something I have to look past. Look at the item for what it is. Will you need it or use it? Can you live without it? Be heartless and rip the memories that are associated with object away from it. In the end, it's just a piece of stuff that will clutter your home. Remember that!

If You Haven't used it in Six Months, Trash it

Another great method that I use to declutter my home is to look at what is before me and evaluate whether or not I have used this item in the past six months. If I haven't used or looked at it that long, I haven't missed it; I then put it into my donation pile. The biggest mistake that you can make is to look at the object and tell yourself that you will use it again. You won't, so don't keep it around. Six months is a reasonable time span to realize whether or not you will use it.

Downsize Your Home

For some of us, we live in a house that is too big for our needs. If possible, downsize your living quarters to something that is more manageable to clean and furnish. I understand that moving is not feasible for all, but if you have the opportunity to downsize your home, you will also be forced to get rid of some of your belongings when you move. Think about it; this might be the way to go!

Downsizing your possessions can be a tough and time-consuming process. No one likes to get rid of their things. After all, you chose them and worked hard to buy them. However, when your life becomes complicated because of your need to maintain your possessions, you're not going to be happy. Try decluttering and downsizing in the area of your possessions and see how much better you feel by making this change.

This is a process so, don't overwhelm yourself with getting rid of all the items you don't need at once. This will make the whole idea seem even more overwhelming than just keeping the stuff in your life. So, I recommend that you take this process in pieces. It could take you a few months to make it through. However long it takes, know that you're making a positive step towards simplifying your life with the shedding of your excess possessions.

Get Rid of Unnecessary Items

If you haven't worn it or used it in six months, get rid of it. The number one cause of clutter is keeping something that we believe that we will use again when in reality, we probably won't. Donate your unworn clothing, shoes, and linens to thrift shops so that they can benefit others. Not only are you solving your clutter problem, but you are also preventing yourself from facing future clutter problems. Plus, you are simplifying your life by being able to know what you have and where it is.

Principle 3: Cleaning areas

1. Kitchen

There is no wrong place to start. Therefore, focus on any part of your kitchen. That might be one drawer; it doesn't matter. It may not sound like a revolutionary idea, but you will build one small success on top of another little success. Eventually, you can make a "mountain" of success.

- Examine the selected drawer. Empty it onto the kitchen table or a countertop.
- Immediately get rid of anything you don't need. Put unnecessary items into donation boxes and garbage

bags.

- Clean the drawer, and sort the items by frequency of use. Arrange things that are used the most frequently in the front part of the drawer.

  - Put the rest of the things behind them. If the drawer is big enough, introducing a drawer divider could also be a help. This bright idea will save your time and energy.

Now, you have to declutter floating shelves in the kitchen

- Place a large sheet on the floor.
- Remove items from your floating shelves, one by one and transfer them to the sheet. In this way, you can see the abundance of stuff in your kitchen.
- You may need to discard or move some items to another room.
- It's time to clean the things that have gotten dusty.
- Place things back on floating shelves. And remember – Balance is the key to a happy kitchen.

Don't overfill your space with a lot of things. Realistically, how many baking dishes, measuring cups or graters do you need? Get rid of the surplus and take back your kitchen!

Next, declutter small kitchen appliances

Before organizing these items, take inventory. How many small appliances do you have? Have you been given a lot of hand-me-downs?

Remove duplicate appliances. For example, if you have two blenders, think about letting one of them go. You can sell these items at a garage sale or donate them to charity.

Ask yourself: Which things do you use most frequently? Divide all the elements into two categories: "rarely use" and "use often."

Therefore, keep only necessary items and purge the rest.

Therefore, try to store what you will use. Keep your small appliances well organized in a kitchen cabinet. This way, when you want to find an individual instrument, you will always know where it is.

Next up: a systematically organized cooking space

You can make the most of your kitchen. Consider how many cabinets you have. Which areas are used for which cooking tasks? How many kitchen appliances and dishes can you eliminate? Perhaps put a detailed plan on paper.

- Bring all cooking utensils and tools together. Toss unwanted cooking tools.
- Put the spices, oils, and bottles of vinegar into designated spots.
- Organize spoons, knives, cutting boards, etc.
- Organize your pots, pans, skillets, and other cookware.

Try to arrange all cookware close to your stove, within easy reach. And from now on, when you want to find your cooking tool, you'll always know where it is.

Prepare your meals in a decluttered kitchen

Cookware such as mixing bowls, cutting boards, kitchen gadgets, knives, and blenders should be organized in a particular area. In this way, they will always be at your fingertips. Cut through the pile of additional kitchen tools that might have accumulated. Get rid of items that don't work. Free up space in your kitchen so that you can enjoy your space to the fullest.

Create a more cook-friendly kitchen

If there is space, create a station on your counter where you will keep your cooking essentials. Cooking oil, salt, black pepper, and garlic are the most commonly used food ingredients. In this way, your space becomes more cook-friendly. Use an old cutting board to designate this spot.

Organize your pots and pans

Empty your kitchen cabinet and utilize it for your pots and pans. Begin by putting the largest pots on the bottom shelf of the cabinet; then, work upwards to the smallest pots and pans. Or store them on an open shelf. Of course, get rid of old and rusty pots and pans and keep only the good ones.

Your pans and pots have unwanted stains? Don't waste your time scrubbing them. You can utilize this great trick and remove the stains quickly and effortlessly. You will need apple peels. Yes, that's it! Add the apple peels to your pan or pot; pour in water; then, allow the water to simmer for about 3 minutes. Then, pour out the water; lastly, cleanse the bowl with a rag.

Another way to keep pots and pans well organized

Countertops are magnets for clutter. Unwashed dishes, utensils, bags, pots, pans, there are too many items there. You can start with all those pots and pans and find a convenient place to store them. Otherwise, you will not be able to cook, bake and eat. If you continue to pile up all these things, your kitchen will descend into an untidy mess.

The most common and the easiest way to organize your pots and pans is to hang them on the wall. If you lack cabinet space, hang up your cookware. Take back your kitchen!

Pot and pan holder

You can quickly build a simple storage area for your favorite cookware. In this case an old pallet would do the trick. To make the pallet look a little bit fancy, you will have to paint It then, anchor it to the wall with drywall screws; lastly, you should add some hooks. And, voila! Your pots and pans with stay neat and tidy.

Don't forget to organize and declutter your knives

There are probably too many knives in your kitchen. Bring all knives together on a kitchen table. Get rid of unwanted ones and organize the good ones. It may be hard to get started, but it saves you work. Here are some suggestions:

- Hang knives on a magnetic strip.
- Consider putting your knives in a designated drawer, but make sure to separate them with drawer dividers.
- A counter-top knife block is also a great solution.

Organize your cutting boards

The old magazine rack is a great storage option. You can install it inside the cabinet door to hold your cutting boards. This is an incredible space saver and a great spot for easy access. Beautiful and tidy!

Solutions for when there is no pantry

Do you live in a small house or an apartment without a pantry? Many apartments are pantry-less, no big deal! You can still make the most of your small kitchen.

- First, get a garbage bag ready and toss the old food and expired items.
- You can designate one or two cupboards in which to store your food.
- To get extra space storage, you can lose the boxes.
- Use baskets to corral small items.
- Try to use space in your refrigerator to the fullest.
- Try to use every nook in the kitchen cabinets.

Organize food in your pantry

Another area to clear will likely be your pantry if you have one. The pantry is one of the biggest clutter magnets in every house.

- First, check out the labels, and read expiration dates carefully.
- Then throw away expired items.
- Donate food items that you do not plan to eat, that no longer fit your dietary regimen or your children refuse to eat.

Here are some useful tips for you.

- Designate a shelf for drinks, coffee, and tea. Put cups and mugs nearby.
- Designate an easy to reach an area with healthy snacks for your children.
- Organize your cupboards so that the items you use most frequently are the most accessible.
- In this way, you can also teach your kids to always put things back in their designated places.

Tips to Clean Your Kitchen

The kitchen is the place which needs to be the cleanest of all other rooms of the house. You cook there and to have the healthy food which you are going to intake needs to be prepared at a clean place. When we see cooking happening at a dirty place, we do not even want to have that same food because it is too tacky and nasty. Well, your house kitchen should always be clean and odorless so that you can enjoy cooking there as well. No one likes to kitchen that is dirty; it does not even feel safe to cook in such a kitchen. You can clean the entire kitchen fully over the weekend so do not wait for once in a year chance to clean the kitchen thoroughly, but it should be cleaned every day.

If you are someone who works and does not have time every day, then it is okay to take out few hours on the weekend to do it yourself. Once you start doing it, you will love it for sure when you see the bright new kitchen which you have cleaned. Over time, you have to maintain the kitchen and the appliances otherwise they stop working. Here are some of the tips which can help you keep the kitchen clean.

1. Empty Sink

If you have a dishwasher, then your life will be easier. Make sure that the dishwasher is empty when you start cooking so that the dirty utensils can simply be rinsed and kept in the dishwasher for washing once you are done cooking. If you do not have a dishwasher, then you could do the same thing but place them in the sink to be washed later.

2. Keep Cleaning

You have to do the cleaning as you continue to cook. If you have to wait for something to be cooked for 10 minutes, then those 10 minutes can be used to wash the dirty dishes. You have to multitask in the kitchen and work faster than you do during your regular routine to make it work.

3. Clean the Sink

When you are done washing the dishes, make sure to clean the sink as well. Take the sponge and the liquid and wipe it all across the pan. Then wash it off so that it can shine. This will ensure that the sink stays clean, and odourless. The grease won't stick to it, and you will have the smooth and shiny sink.

4. Maintenance

If you see something is not working in the kitchen, then get it fixed as soon as possible. Do it on your off day or over the weekend so that you can keep it maintained. If you do not get it fixed, then it will keep on getting worse which will get you even a bigger expense over the period. For instance, if you feel that the tap water is coming out too slow, then you need to get it fixed so that it does not stop giving you the water one day. When you repair the problem immediately it starts, then you do not have to go through the bigger problem.

5. Oil the boards

Do you love to put on the boards, and then oil them once in a while so that it does not take the appearance of broken wood? Well, when the wood gets busted, it is likely to be cut at one time. This can save you money, and you will not have to replace the item as well.

6. Have the cleaning tools

If you have the right cleaning tools for the kitchen, then you will be quickly cleaning it once in a while. Suppose that you feel like cleaning the kitchen and you do not have the proper floor cleaner, yet you do not feel like you want to go out there to get the tools. If you entertain this feeling, you will definitely not do any cleaning. For this reason, ensure that you have all the cleaning tools for the various places (the floor, oven, microwave, countertop and much more) when you go shopping.

7. Keep less stuff visible

It will be better if you keep the utensils and everything in the cabinets. Make certain that there is nothing placed on the countertop before you go bed; the kitchen should be neat and tidy without any food or even a plate sitting on the countertop. If you leave the food outside, most likely the insects will be attracted to it, and they will invade your kitchen in the night time when you will be sleeping which can compromise the hygiene of your kitchen.

8. Recycling Bin

Make sure to have a trash bin where you can throw the trash. Also, to avoid crawling insects and a foul smell from the trash, ensure that you empty the bin regularly and clean it on a daily basis.

9. Cooking tips

Make sure that when you are cooking, you do not throw everything lying around the kitchen. Try to cook food in a simple and quick manner. After cooking, you will definitely be tired, and all you will want to do is just have some food to eat and rest. For this reason, make certain that you clean up as you continue cooking; this will ensure that no dirty dishes pile up during this whole process. Also, if you regularly use the oven and microwave, make sure that you clean up every other weekend to get rid of disease causing bacteria or germs.

10. Develop a habit of Cleaning up

It is important that you develop the habit of cleaning because having a dirty kitchen is not so nice. No one will like it, and it will cause trouble for you one day because there won't be hygiene involved. When you have a clean kitchen, you feel good, and you want to cook delicious food for your family. You do not have to clean the kitchen to show someone but for yourself and the hygiene. The sooner you develop this habit, the better it will be for you because it is not hard to do but necessary to do.

2. Bathroom

The bathroom needs a systematic plan for organizing and decluttering. Divide your space into three zones and clear out every bit of your bathroom. Putting your bathroom items back is as easy as ABC. Afterwards, prepare a relaxing bath and enjoy!

Start by considering the bigger picture.

First of all, you have to set up individual spots for certain items. What to do further? Of course, you should buy particular organizing products. Or you can make them yourself. Just make sure to buy ones that match the décor of your space. For example, you can use plastic containers for your bathroom, but you will not use them for your living room with solid wood furniture. You can put some plastic items in kids' rooms, too. It is important to make a difference and consider the aesthetics. If you have no idea what to purchase and find this difficult, stick to a basic rule – The simpler, the better! Once you've bought a new organizing product, use it to improve your life. And you will wonder how you ever got along without them!

Decluttering missions for the entire bathroom

- Take the 10-10-10 challenge! This would mean:
- Ten items to be repaired and returned to the positions to which they belong;
- Ten items to throw away;
- Ten items to donate

It will be an exciting way to organize 30 things in your bathroom right now. This challenge is an incredibly fun step to take so that children will join you willingly. What's the best of all? This problem will become an entertaining competition between your kids. Keep this tip in your back pocket and use it every time your bathroom is a total mess. In fact, you can use this trick in any part of your house. The principles remain the same.

Let dust be your guide!

Do you have trouble organizing the bathroom's limited space? Do you need that comb with missing teeth? What about that fraying toothbrush? Realistically, your bathroom is an activity-intensive room. Accessing shower gel, soap, shampoo or conditioner can be annoying when they aren't stored at your fingertips. First of all, take a black plastic garbage bag and throw away broken items, valueless products, empty bottles, and so on; half-used products as well. If you haven't used that lotion for six months or the past year, you probably never will. Here is a simple trick – dust can be your guide. It means any product with a dusty coating goes to the trash right now!

Next, use a box that is designated as a "donate box" for unused surplus products that are still useful. The whole process will take less than 15 minutes. Declutter your bathroom once and for all!

A systematic plan for your bathroom

Try to divide your space into three zones.

- The first zone is designated for everyday items, e.g., soap, toothbrushes, shampoo, shower gel, and razor. This zone should be user-friendly and very accessible. Store these items on the countertop, in the top drawer, or in hanging baskets.
- The second zone holds elements that are used weekly and monthly, e.g., makeup, perfumes, nail care equipment. Store them in the middle drawer and on the toilet-top storage cupboard, taking care to give the items easily accessible spots.
- The third zone is designated for the items that are rarely used. It includes under-sink space and the shelf above the bathroom door.

Keep your bathroom clutter-free and sparkling!

There are a lot of products that can make your bathroom sparkle. For example, you could use household cleaning cloths, wipes, mops, cleaning brushes, scouring pads, glass cleaners, microfiber cloths, etc. However, all of these small products could make clutter because they never have their designated place. And you still have a mess in the bathroom.

Your goal is to clean and organize your bathroom in a short time so that you can get on with the more important and fun things in your life. The solution is easier than you think. Add a tension rod underneath a bathroom cabinet to maximize space. Then, hang "S-hooks" for storing your cleaning products as well as the other bathroom supplies. You can also add a second tension rod for even more space.

End your day with a clean bathroom cabinet

Is there anything better than walking into a clean space? Get this done today and you will be happier in the evening. This easy task will affect your mood for the rest of your day for sure. Ready, set, go!

- First of all, take everything out of the cabinet.
- Then wipe down the interior and shelves.
- Have a trash bag on hand and toss unwanted items. Dispose of everything that you haven't used in the last year and everything that is empty and nearly empty.
- Create your shopping list. In this way, you'll be able to simplify the clutter so that you can enjoy your bathroom to the fullest.

Cut clutter in the bathroom – shower and bath caddies

Personal hygiene products are scattered all over your bathroom. And you have all that mess! Keeping your bathroom tidy and organized can be challenging. However, with determination, you can win this battle.

Your favorite moisturizers, lotions, deodorants and other products can be cleverly sorted out and stored. Try hanging a bath caddy on a hook mounted on the wall, and the problem is solved! Shower and bath caddies will help remove the floor of your bathroom. Therefore, install this great item close to your bathtub or hang it in your shower cabin, and take a shower right now! You can use bath caddies to keep your makeup, too. After decluttering, prepare a relaxing bath and enjoy!

Under the bathroom sink

Are you embarrassed to let anyone come into your bathroom? Is your bathroom sink cabinet jammed with unwanted items? There is no doubt – clutter can influence the way you live. Here are simple hacks for clearing out your bathroom sink cabinet.

- Take everything out and lay it on a sheet.
- Throw out or recycle everything that is broken and useless.
- Wipe down your bathroom sink cabinet.
- Reorganize your products by categories. Use baskets to keep them neat and tidy. Your bathroom will be in order, and you will be happy!

Under-the-sink storage ideas

Here are some creative ideas to organize useful space under your sink.

- Keep your cleaning supplies and tools in an easy-to-grab basket so you can take it out every time you start cleaning.
- Fill another basket with boxes of tissue or extra toilet paper.
- Hang spray bottles on a tension rod.
- Place large-sized items such as toilet brush and bottles in the back.

Bright and practical: over-the-door bin

An easy way to store more in your bathroom

Tired of wasting time searching for a bath item you need? A shoe holder is a simple but great organizer that can be used in many different ways. The possibilities are endless. You can attach a shoe holder to the inside of a bathroom cabinet. And you will get extra storage for your bottles, cleaners, spray bottles, cosmetic products, and so on. Catch clutter and reorganize your bathroom! Happiness indeed!

Keep your beauty products neat and tidy in a small bathroom

Do you feel as though your bathroom is too small? Well, this is a problem faced by all who fail to get rid of all unwanted and unnecessary products and tools.

Now you should designate spots for every bathroom item. Make a use of every nook in your bathroom by hanging baskets or bags with handles on stylish hooks. It's best to purchase uniform hanging baskets to enhance the aesthetic effect.

Floating shelves – a brilliant idea for a small bathroom

Use floating shelves to create extra storage in your small bathroom. They are perfect for stashing extra towels and other items. The benefits are obvious; you will use every inch, and space will be clutter-free at the same time. Floating shelves fit in narrow spaces, and they can corral a lot of bathroom essentials.

Three storage tricks for a tiny bathroom

- Save space by stacking your products in a decorative magazine holder. It is a thin and useful organizer.
- Hang your hairdryer and hair curlers on adhesive hooks inside a bathroom cabinet door.
- Organize your bottles, deodorants, and lotions on an old wine rack. You can paint the frame and get a stylish organizer. These original tricks will leave you feeling great and refreshed.

A quick way to clean your medicine cabinet

Create one spot for drugs. First, get rid of outdated stuff and used items such as old creams, expired ointments and drugs, as well as all drugs that did not have any effect on your health problems. Get rid of "just in case" items because these things take up space, and, honestly, they weigh us down. Therefore, free up your space for more beautiful things than medical supplies.

A cheap and smart way to store bath toys

Bathtub toys can create a huge muddle in your bathroom. If they are scattered all over the bathroom, it's time for a change.

You can only hang a multilevel fruit basket for additional storage. Take advantage of vertical storage, and you will declutter your bathroom instantly. A fruit basket can be used as a caddy so that water drains out, and the toys are easy for your child to reach. This idea works for kid's shampoo, sponges, and other bath accessories. Try to hang the fruit basket in an unused corner. Put bath toys into the basket, and you will keep all the toys in one place. If you have a tiny bathroom, it will save a lot of space. Brilliant!

A magnetic strip – organize small metal grooming items

Nail clippers, tweezers, bobby pins, hairpins and other small metal items are scattered everywhere in your bathroom. Tired of searching for them?

You can add a magnetic strip to the inside of a medicine cabinet or other storage area. It's up to you!

- You can buy a magnetic tape at any home improvement store.
- Then, you should cut a magnetic strip to fit your medicine cabinet; peel away the cover on the video side.
- Arrange your small metal items.

An intelligent solution for toilet paper

If you purchase toilet rolls in bulk, you probably have a problem with storing them. How about using shoe bags? Put the bags in the bathroom closet, and that's it. Clever!

Organize a complete makeup (Part I)

Are you a makeup addict? Do you spend money buying duplicates for beauty products you already have because you can't find them? Are your products scattered all over the bathroom? Even a small number of beauty products can make your bathroom look cluttered. If you feel helpless because you can't solve the problem, you are not alone. There is a solution. Follow these few steps, and you will sort out your makeup products quickly and effortlessly.

Ready, set, go!

- It's time to start throwing out the unwanted products. Gather up all of your beauty products. Check expiration dates.
- Try your best to minimize the number of beauty products in your home. If you can't remember the last time you used a beauty product, ask yourself, "Can I see myself using this again?"
- Clean up your beauty products.
- After that, you should choose a convenient place to store your favorite products.

And from now on, when you want to find some beauty product, you'll always know where it is. Lovely!

Organize a complete makeup (Part II)

You buy all kinds of makeup products because they make you look and feel better, right? Do you keep your makeup and beauty products well organized? If your makeup is a mess, you can't enjoy it to the fullest. One of the best solutions to keep your makeup organized is a drawer with dividers. Group makeup products in a way that is logical to you. Toss unwanted makeup. Determine how to organize best what's left by grouping your beauty products by type and frequency of use. Enjoy doing your makeup!

An ingenious idea for storing your small beauty products

Are your makeup products like eyeshadow, mascara, and lipstick scattered all over the bathroom cabinet?

Put your everyday small beauty products into an easily accessible spot. Consider using a jewelry organizer to store all these little items. If you lack cabinet space, this will be a great idea for you! And from now on, when you want to find your favorite mascara or lipstick, you'll always know where it is.

A cookie jar and a cupcake tray in your bathroom

Out of sight means less visual clutter, but things hidden in the bathroom cabinet tend to be forgotten.

Here are two amazing and chip hacks for decluttering and organizing bathroom accessories, makeup, etc. Make them visible and easily accessible. You can use a clear cookie jar to store your lip glosses or nail polishes. Then, you can stack your makeup products on the tiers of a cupcake tray. In this way, you can group them by categories.

Change your habits – change your bathroom

Duplication of bathroom stuff is demanding a lot of your hard-earned money. Group items in a way that is logical to you. Designate a spot for all your duplicates and extras. A plastic container works well. When you run out of any product, check that bottle to see if you already have it on hand.

Personalized bathroom shelves

If you have space on the wall, consider installing personalized boxes. You will have a cute storage box for each family member. You can store items your family uses most frequently so they should be easily reachable. You can paint these shelves so each family member will have her/his favorite color. Cute!

Organize your nail polish

You love nail polishes; there are dozens of them. They are scattered all over the house. And you know why? If you have an old spice rack, you will find an ideal home for your nail polishes. You can also store essential oils and perfumes there. You may want to paint this spice rack using a color of choice. Another idea is to display your perfume bottles on top of a cake stand.

How to organize your drawers once and for all?

Often wonder how bathroom drawers get so messy?

- First, take the drawers out and empty them. Assemble all items. Check expiration dates and examine every piece. Ask yourself, "Can I see myself using this again? If not, simply throw it away.
- Clean up your drawers.
- Then, you can decorate them by coating the inside with wallpaper cut to fit. Use drawer dividers and smart, clear bins to take the organization to the next level!

Solve overstuffed drawers

With the right setup, there's a place for every bathroom item.

After decluttering, create three piles:

1. Things that should go in the drawer;
2. Stuff that shouldn't go in;
3. Clutter and garbage.

Deal with the confusion immediately and group necessary items by category. For example, tuck your hairdryer and other corded appliances in a basket; then put the basket into a cleared drawer. Put the rest of your items back in place using baskets. As you can see, the solution is simpler than you thought.

Use a utensil tray for your favorite beauty products

Are your tweezers, lipsticks, mascara, makeup brushes, and the other beauty products scattered around your bathroom? Place the utensil tray in a drawer in the bathroom to keep these items organized. This is useful for all these small things that every girl has in her life. Create your beauty zone without any investment. Lovely!

Organize your hair accessories

You are doing your hair, and you need some bobby pins urgently. Where are the thousands of bobby pins you bought? Hair clips, hair grips, barrettes, hair bands… there are too many items. This is a budget-friendly way to organize your favorite cheap but valuable small items. You will need zero dollars!

You can clean an old shoe box and use it for all your hair trinkets. Cover the box with wrapping paper of choice. And Voila! Bask in the glory of your new lifestyle!

A fun way to organize trinkets

Girls love jewellery ; earrings, bracelets, necklaces, etc. Yours or your daughter's costume jewelry deserves a special "home." However, it does not have to be an expensive box or jewelry holder. You can use mason jars! You can also add some labels to group your jewelry. Then, you can paint your jars, wrap a fancy ribbon around them, and lace and tinsel. You will have excellent and inexpensive jewelry storage. At the same time, you will have fun decorating your jars.

Hair ties, ponytail holders, and headbands

For everyday hairstyles, make sure you're stocked up on essential hair accessories. Nevertheless, they tend to get lost in various areas of the house. And they create clutter! Realistically, how many of those trinkets do you need? Therefore, get rid of old and useless headbands and ties.

You can use an oatmeal container for hair accessories storage. Or you can purchase an inexpensive decorative bin for that purpose.

3. Dining Room

Declutter your dining room cabinet

You need to find space for your porcelain dinnerware sets, tablecloths, candles, expensive glasses, napkins and other items. Dining storage allows you to keep everything neat and tidy. However, if it is jammed with clutter, you probably waste your time searching for an individual item. Luckily, there is an excellent way to declutter dining room cabinets.

1. Take everything out including cabinet organizers like shelf dividers. It will help you to see the available space in the enclosure.
2. Wipe down your cabinet and remove dust and spills.
3. This is the fun part. You should make six piles – "keep in office," "put away in another place," "giveaway," "sell," "trash," and "recycle (repurpose)."

Keep in mind – small appliances are fun to shop for, but after a while, most of them seem to disappear into the darkness of your cabinet. Some of them have emotional significance, but you don't use them, and they just gather dust. Resolve this sentiment and throw away all these unwanted and useless things.

Now, you are ready to organize your dining room cabinet.

Keep your dining room cabinet organized

First, you should find a place for things you use every day. They should be at your fingertips. If you have limited space in your cabinet, remove rarely used items to another place in the house. In this way, you can easily organize your casual dinnerware and everyday items such as a tablecloth, napkins, cutlery, etc.

Sort by category: for example, 1) napkins and napkin rings; 2) cutlery, etc.

Now, you only need to maintain this new clutter-free environment you've created. Bravo!

How to maintain a decluttered dining room?

Yes, the clutter defines a part of you as a person. For example, if you love magazines or books, these things reflect your passions, and this is quite reasonable. If you enjoy browsing through magazines in your dining room, this is quite reasonable, too. But you should be organized. Do not leave magazines scattered on the dining table. How to maintain a decluttered dining room?

- Try to spend ten minutes each evening clearing out everything that doesn't belong in your dining room.
- Then each time you plan to buy something new for your dining room, search through your drawers and cabinets, so you do not buy duplicates.
- It is important to sort through your dining room cabinets at the start of each season.

Declutter the dining room table

Any clutter tends to accumulate on your dining room table if kitchen accessories and other items don't have a designated place where they are stored. So take the time to clear off your table.

1. Assemble all objects and start sorting them into three categories: "kitchen accessories," "other accessories," and "dining room accessories." It will take less than 10 minutes.
2. Now you need to find a spot for every item. Put away things that do not belong here. Things that belong in the kitchen take to the kitchen. The other things will need their "homes" in the other parts of the house.
3. Arrange items from the third category and keep them

organized on your dining table. Afterwards, to maintain a clear dining table, you will need to find homes for all the things that seem to accumulate on your dining table. That's all you've got to do.

Promote beauty and order

Retake the valuable surface of your dining table with this simple hack. You could try place something pretty, such as a flower arrangement, on the dining table. This will do the trick for you as it discourages people from placing all sorts of extraneous things on your table.

Corral kids' belongings

If your children use the dining table for board games and homework, it's no big deal. However, that's not its primary purpose. Teach them to clear the supplies off after each session. Then they should store their belongings in a designated place. It is significant for small items such as toy bricks and blocks, pencils and the other school supplies to be kept under control. In fact, the best solution is to set up desks or a work table for those activities.

Dining room organization – baskets

If you find you can't use your dining room for what it is meant for, it's time to solve this problem. There are a lot of reasons why you should use your dining room more frequently. The family dining room is more than just a place to eat. This is the area where the family can sit down together and socialize with one another, and enjoy gatherings with family and friends. However, if your dining room is jammed with stuff, it cannot serve its purpose.

Baskets are perfect organization tools for this kind of room. You can keep a lot of things in them. In that way, you will remove clutter from table, chairs and display cabinets. If your dining room is filled with knick-knacks, candles, lighters, napkins, and other small items, consider buying beautiful straw baskets. You can go one step further and purchase baskets with handles to hang them on a wall with hooks.

Use a dresser in your dining room

The dresser is a super organizing piece of furniture. You can find an old table or even an antique one at garage sales.

Now you can keep silverware, china, linens, candles, hand wipes and other things well organized. You can divide and place items in categories based on the frequency of use. For example, designate drawers for the following categories:

- napkins,
- tablecloths,
- Disposable dishes,
- placemats, etc.

Keep your sideboard neat and tidy

Those coasters, china, stemware, silverware and bottle openers you place on your sideboard should be organized in a tidy manner. This piece of furniture is designed to hold a lot of diverse items, making it perfect for your dining room.

How do I keep my sideboard organized for you to enjoy your dining room to the fullest?

- Set aside some time, e.g., on Saturday morning, after family breakfast. Remove everything from the sideboard and put it together. Toss damaged broken and useless things. Donate duplicates and things that you will never use again.
- Then wipe down your sideboard and remove dust and spills. Clean and polish each item.
- Create groups for all the things you will put back on the sideboard. Designate a spot for each group of articles.

Decide how to store them: vertically or horizontally. Arrange your items and enjoy the new look of your sideboard!

Your cocktail cabinet

Do you like cocktails and romantic dinners? Are your spirits and liquor bottles distributed all over the kitchen and dining room? If your answer is yes – consider a cocktail cabinet.

- Sort items into categories.
- Assign a space for your mixers, ice buckets, shakers, trays, and other cocktail party equipment.
- Designate a space for the bottles and group them into categories. d. Line the shelves with paper or cork lining and place your glasses on them. Keep drinks upright and in widely spaced rows.

Extra storage – rolling bar cart

Wheeled furniture is always a great solution, especially for small spaces. If you need extra counter space, consider buying a vehicle. You can organize everything simply and practically.

You can also transport your dishes from kitchen to dining room using this cart. You can find a metal cart with glass and bottle support. A small rolling bar cart is just what you need to make things more manageable. And you can place your vehicle anywhere you want.

You get a lot of extra storage with hanging shelves

There are a lot of things that we use on a daily basis. Especially if we have kids. Parents are aware of it. However, at the top of most parents' lists is clearing clutter from your dining room by neatly organizing pile of toys, newspapers, books, groceries and other items that are spread out all over the dining room.

Are you looking for a daily activity organizer? What about floating shelves? Floating shelves are inexpensive and practical solutions for your dining room. They are easy to install, and you can find them in modern colors and different sizes depending on their purpose. The possibilities are endless.

Sort your newspapers and magazines

You love your magazines so much. However, do you have magazine holders? Or do you have a special home for them, for example, on a bookshelf? If your answer is No, it's time to sort your favorite magazines. Here are a few steps to do that quickly and effortlessly.

- Decide which magazines you need to keep. If your answer is – "I probably should read these," get them out of your house.
- If you need to read some magazines for work assignments or your kids need some of them for school, you can keep them.
- Therefore, you should sort them out and put them in the designated place. A good solution is to purchase a couple of magazine racks.

Wheeled furniture for a small living space

This is a life hack that can help you to declutter fast and easy.

Wheeled tables, desks, and wastebaskets offer the advantage of being easily moved. You can even find ottomans, side tables, and chairs on wheels. They are perfect for a cramped space because they can easily be repositioned.

How to throw a dinner party in a small apartment?

You have a small dining room, or you don't have that space at all, but you love parties. Don't let a small space hold you back! Here are some tricks to make it a snap.

- A living room with the furniture moved out of the way can make a great space for your dinner party.
- Use folding chairs that can be easily replaced. Your guests can sit on pillows, why not?!
- If you can't make a dining table work in your living room, throw a cocktail party with appetizers. To serve, use large platters on a coffee table as well as carts and wheeled furniture.

Weeknight dinner party – keep party supplies on hand

It's time to declutter your party supplies. Toss everything that is broken and useless. You can use a large-sized shoe box and label it "Party Box."

Your party box will include balloons, candles, streamers, etc. And you'll have peace of mind knowing that you're well prepared.

Then, choose your favorite party recipes and enjoy the fun. There is a money saving hack: remember to shop sales after the holidays. Prices for party supplies are the lowest at this time.

4. Bedroom

Get rid of unwanted items and opt for small pieces of furniture. You will free up your space significantly! It might seem like a daunting task, but you can start with baby steps. Declutter one area at a time and don't move to the next zone until you have finished the previous one.

It is such a relief and joy to have all those items finally sorted! Get your bedroom in tip-top shape!

Get organized – divide into zones

As you probably know, it's easy to let a room descend into chaos. Use these simple rules to streamline your bedroom. One of the best methods to tackle the problem is to divide your room into three areas: 1) the sleeping zone; 2) the relaxing and entertaining area; 3) the grooming area. Also, many of us have the fourth part, and it is the work area.

Everything in your bedroom should fit into one of these three or four categories. If you have an item that doesn't fit, it may not belong in your bedroom.

Declutter your bedroom – surplus furniture

Is your room jammed with furniture? Having too many chairs, tables, dressers, and other things makes the bedroom appear smaller.

- Get rid of surplus furniture to create more space. Think about what you can sell or donate. You can sell it at a garage sale, or you can give it away. You should only keep the pieces that are necessary for your bedroom to function. Remember – less is more!
- Clean your room thoroughly.
- The way you arrange furniture can make a big difference. Find a spot for every piece that makes the most sense to you.
- Add a new decoration, maybe a picture. Enjoy your new bedroom.

Handy tips to help declutter your bedroom

1. While you are going through this mess, ask yourself: Do I need all these things in my room? Is anything in this area not being used? Toss unwanted items.
2. This is the fun part. You should make six piles – keep, put away in another place, give away, sell, trash, and recycle (repurpose). If there are items that could be useful to someone, give them away.
3. Designate a spot for every item. Put things back in their places.

To maintain this streamlined environment, stick to a few important rules:

- Make your bed every morning.
- Keep your clothes organized. Place them in your closet or the laundry basket.
- Avoid bedside clutter.
- Do not ruin what you have achieved.

Turn a dresser into bedside tables

There are a lot of random items under your bed, on the floor and all over the bedroom. You can replace your side tables with small dressers and get some extra storage for all your small items and tchotchkes. Of course, this trick will not spoil the aesthetics of the room.

Use the advantage of hidden storage

If you are looking for a place to keep your sports equipment, blankets, nighttime necessities and other things, a wicker trunk is a perfect solution. This cute hidden storage has plenty of space, and it also gives the bedroom an elegant decorative effect and evokes a homey feel.

Turn bedroom clutter into décor

If lots of items are littering your floor, you can artfully arrange them. You can stack your big fat books and create a nice décor touch. You can organize magazines in the same fashion. This is a little change, but it can transform your bedroom. It will bring such relief and happiness to have them finally sorted!

Rolling cart for your bedroom

If you are wondering how to live a more organized life, here's a simple hack. Use a rolling cart in your room!

This fantastic vehicle can be used as a bedside table. Consider buying the car with a drawer so you can keep jewelry, keys, and other favorites well organized. This cart can also hide everyday clutter. The possibilities are endless, so be creative!

Small furniture will open up your space

No matter how big your bedroom is, opt for small pieces of furniture, and you will free up your space significantly. It's better to have a few pieces with drawers and a few floating shelves than a large closet. In this way, you will achieve better results because every item will find their "home." In the large closet, they could be scattered and invisible.

Get organized: use dividers

All these small items create a lot of clutter in your bedroom. It might seem like a daunting task, but you can start with baby steps. Luckily, there are drawer dividers to keep all items neat and tidy. You can also use small dishes such as vintage cups. Don't throw your accessories into a large drawer once you get home. Divide the drawers and put every item back into a designated spot. Get your bedroom in tip-top shape!

Hang instead of stand

You can hang a wicker basket to save space in your bedroom. You can use this basket for your socks, slippers, scarves, mittens, etc. This is a perfect spot for items that we usually throw somewhere in the bedroom once we get home.

Organization hacks for your tiny bedroom

You have a little bedroom. Fortunately, there are a lot of great tricks to make the most of your room.

Consider buying a console table. It will be used as a shelf and a desk. This is a perfect place for your morning coffee, magazines, a book, glasses, etc. And you will feel good. Feeling good can be a way of life.

Maximizing under-bed storage

It is a great place to keep an alarm clock, your magazines, books, reading glasses, tissues, and so on. You will have more usable space in your bedroom. And of course, some things will be hidden, so they do not spoil the aesthetics of the room. Great!

Turn your desk into a bedside table

You do not have to have a large bedroom to be happy. Balance is the key to a comfortable bedroom. Don't overfill your space with a lot of things. Here's a hack that will save a lot of space. Just place your desk next to the bed, and you will get two in one!

Clear up your bedroom and sleep peacefully.

Within the walls of our home, we try to live a balanced life. The key to a balanced life is organization. The bedroom allows us to express our creativity through organizing and decorating. Regarding creativity, do you need a footboard? If you have a tiny bedroom, it can be an entirely unnecessary piece of furniture. Therefore, put your desk there instead of the footboard. Great idea!

Remember – Take control of your clutter! Everyone can designate five minutes a day to putting things away. Remove anything that doesn't belong in the bedroom and go to sleep. Use every corner in your tiny bedroom.

If you don't have a closet in the room, you can hang your clothes on a tension rod. You can also hang towels and other items. If you are a fan of simplicity, this is the right solution for you. And when you want to find some item, you will always know where it is.

Declutter and organize your relaxing zone

Is your relaxing area jammed with items, so you are not able to relax there? Organization of the relaxing area requires tidying, cleaning, and sorting to make your space a calming haven. You can tackle this problem with a few simple hacks!

- Gather decluttering tools such as garbage boxes and bags. Bring all items together and sort them. Create six piles: keep, put away in another place, give away, sell, trash, and recycle (repurpose). Sort each item into one of the piles. Work systematically around the entire space.
- Toss unwanted items.
- Take a duster and clean your ornaments, lamps, vases and other elements such as guitars, painting equipment, books, etc.
- Get it tidy! Put everything back and enjoy the new look of your bedroom. To soften this area, organize your pillows. There's nothing more beautiful than waking up to a clean space.

Under bed boxes and storage to save your space

Sometimes you do not know where to put large items such as coats, blankets, bed sets and similar things. There is a lot of space under your bed, right? A large box with blankets, duvet covers, pillows, and bedding sets could fit there.

You can keep things like winter clothes in under bed storage boxes. Therefore, these items stay out of your way, but they're still close at hand. Give it a try and keep your room in tip-top shape!

Declutter the work zone

It is the time to organize the place where you do homework, study or work. Here are some guidelines:

- Bring all items together. You should have four garbage bags: keep, give away, sell, and trash. Sort each item into one of the piles.

- Then throw unwanted items away. Toss everything that is broken, rusty, useless, etc.
- It's not enough for your workspace to be tidy – it must be clean, too. Take a duster and clean your stuff.
- Put everything back and enjoy your new desk. Remember – you can turn your workspace into a clutter-free paradise!

Change your habits - change your workspace for the better

Your penholder contains a lot of pencils, but only one pen works. And many of your pencils need replacing. Then you have a lot of junk mail on your desk. Your penholder is old and dusty. So you need to start throwing out the old paper, boxes, pencils, and so on. Otherwise, there will be no space for you in this room. Clutter makes you confused and distracted. Scientists believe that a huge number of things that make you happy are within your control.

So, easily help yourself. Close your eyes breathe deeply and visualize a neat and tidy workspace. Enjoy your visualization for a few minutes. Focus on the result – productivity without stress and confusion. Feel happiness and calmness. It will increase your chances of decluttering your desk right now. By practicing this mental exercise for 5 to 6 minutes a day, you will be happy to put your office in order at the end of each working day. Make a list of your obligations for the next day, and you will form a new healthy habit. Good luck!

One of the best organizers of all time – command hooks

Attach hooks on the wall next to the desk, and you'll get extra storage space for your workspace. Hang your backpacks, laptop bag, purse, and the other bags that you need for work. Be inspired by command hooks!

There are lots of ways to use command hooks. Here's some of them:

- You can use two hooks to make wrapping paper easy to tear. It can be a great solution for adhesive tapes, too.
- Then hang a wire file box on the side of your desk.
- You can use special hooks for holding cords.
- You can design a paper towel holder with two hooks and a spare wire.

Baskets for your work zone

Here's a great hack for your work area, especially for those with a little workspace – Use hooks to hang baskets on the wall! You can use old wire baskets and paint them to add vintage charm to your space. This trick makes your everyday job beautiful! Of course, this system will be easy to maintain because your items are in sight. You will be so happy that your little workspace has clean surfaces and a bit of personality.

Desk makeover – never enough baskets

Position buckets on the side of your craft table or work desk and you'll get extra space storage for your small items. Add baskets to hold your necessities and trinkets. You will have all these items at your fingertips, and the desk will be clutter-free! And remember – it must be inspiring!

Think outside the shelf

Turn your wire storage baskets on their sides, attach them to the wall, and you've got stunning shelves! Turn boring wire baskets into functional storage solutions. These unconventional shelves are both fun and practical.

Use empty cans to create your desk organizer

There is no doubt – clutter can influence the way you think and work. If you are looking for an easy way to organize your home office here's a simple hack for freeing up your workspace.

You can use empty cans for pencils, markers, rulers, scissors, adhesive tapes and other useful items. All you have to do is to clean up a few tin cans and cover them with a trendy color of your choice. And you get the original desk organizer!

A high-level organization – rolling cart

If you have lots of small items at your workstation a rolling cart is a right solution. There is another huge advantage – this vehicle is small enough to fit under your desk. You can place it in a corner, too. And you will be able to transfer it wherever you want. Lovely!

Maximize storage space in your workstation

This is an inexpensive and straightforward solution for a cluttered workspace. You will use wall space and free up the rest of the workspace. Consider installing freestanding wall units and liberating your workstation.

Create a spot for incoming papers

You used to have piles and piles of incoming papers; various notices, receipts, manuals, flyers, warranties and the other documents. The whole family, including you, put them in different spots and they are distributed all over the house – on the kitchen table, on the dresser in the hallway, on the counter, etc. Your car is also not any better as you have placed documents of all kinds there as well. So you can't find anything! Stop battling with the paper clutter once and for all!

Designate an inbox tray in a precise location of your home. Put every paper into that inbox tray. Got some papers? Put it into your inbox. Done! This is only a little change, but it can completely transform your paperwork. It will be such a relief to have it finally sorted!

You can quickly sort the files

A mountain of paperwork is a nightmare for many people. This happens because you haven't created a good spot for papers that keep piling up for days, weeks, months... No worries, the solution is at your fingertips. You can organize some simple folders.

First of all, you should bring the papers all together. Only go throughout all rooms in your house and pick up any bits of paper.

Bring them into one place. Now you have your pile of papers.

Next, create the folders.

Then, add labels. For instance, you can make labels named "Bills." Or "Trash." Or "Papers requiring action" (e.g., forms, school papers, etc.)

Take a handful of papers from the pile. You should make quick decisions: file them right now or trash them. That's it!

Solve cable-clutter problem

Organizing your cables is a never-ending battle. You probably don't want a bunch of wires hanging down there. However, there is a simple trick. Rain gutters are the cheap solution. Set up your creative cable management under your desk and enjoy! Go to your local home center or hardware store and pick up a rain gutter. You will also need some accessories to install it.

Of course, you can buy a cable organizer and solve the problem quickly. Get your cables under control today!

A shoe organizer can help you to organize your craft supplies

You have a vast collection of art supplies, right? However, they are falling on the floor of your room; they are chucked to the back end. There is a simple trick for that. A plastic Over-the-Door shoe organizer is your solution! It is perfect for storing all these small items.

Hang a shoe organizer on the door of your room or the closet.

Put your craft supplies in their seats.

Pegboard for your small tools

You can add a pegboard to your workspace to maximize vertical space. In this way, you will have quick access to the frequently used tools.

- First, purchase the pegboard of choice.
- To take this project to the next level, paint your pegboard in your favorite color.
- Next, install the pegboard in your workspace. Installing a pegboard is a quick and inexpensive way to improve your workspace.
- Keep your workspace safe, organized and beautiful by storing your frequently used tools on your pegboard. Have fun!

5. Living Room

Organizing hacks for a clutter-free living room

There is no doubt that even a few extra items can create mess and clutter in your living room, especially if it is a tiny space. How to declutter your living room? There are a few basic tips:

Get rid of unwanted items. As you work through the items in your living room, here are two important questions to keep in mind: Is this useful? Is this beautiful? Now throw out any clutter that is lying around. Get rid of surplus furniture, too.

Decide on the purpose. Ask yourself: What is the function of this piece of furniture? Think about what you can sell or donate. You can sell unwanted items at a garage sale, or you can give them away. You should only keep the pieces that are necessary for your living room to function, and to be comfortable. Clean your room thoroughly.

Reorganize your items. Find a spot for every item that makes the most sense to you.

It's important to maintain this new clutter-free environment you've created. Once a week, you should take some time to clean this space of dust and dirt. Remember – it gets easier with time!

Go a step further.

Are magazines, kids' items, and office supplies scattered all over your living room? Sick and tired of cleaning and organizing? It seems like a never-ending job. Happily, there are simple life hacks to keep clutter under control.

Step one: Savvy furniture. Try to choose functional furniture that doubles as extra space storage. For example, you could use a coffee table with a lower shelf or benches with hidden storage such as a lift-up cover.

Step two: There is no doubt that the living room is the most frequented room in every house. For that reason, it is a catch-all for clutter! Now, you should remove excess ornaments and plants. During this phase, toss unwanted decorations, threadbare rugs, broken things, and other useless items. Please be practical with every item.

Step three: Think twice before you start purchasing organizers. Is there something else that you can throw away? It's so important to ensure you have enough storage space to organize everything. Remember – less is more!

Now, doesn't that feel better?

Straightforward and traditional living room storage ideas

Despite the size of your room, you are looking for ideas to save space and make the room look organized and clutter-free. There are a lot of ways to organize your things in the living room.

- An open shelf is one of the most familiar pieces of furniture.
- You can use different kinds of dressers and sideboards.
- Cabinets are irreplaceable when it's a question of storage.
- Next solution is lots of cute baskets.
- Display cabinets with their snazzy design are always in vogue.

The possibilities are endless so choose what suits you!

Ideas for organizing your open shelving

Open shelving is a very good idea to add some much-needed organization to your living room. Follow these simple rules to keep your living room ship-shape.

- Preparation. First and foremost, make sure you'll have enough space. If you are not sure, consider buying adjustable shelving.
- Categorization. Group items by category. Put like with like.
- Imagination. Invest in suitable containers such as decorative wire baskets or old buckets. Let your imagination run wild!
- Presentation. Display your favorites like family heirlooms and photographs. However, be careful not to overcrowd your shelves.

A cozy living room makeover – dressers

A dresser serves as a perfect closet alternative or as an ideal supplemental living room storage unit. How to organize your dresser? Here are a few rules.

Free up your space. Get a jump start on your dresser. As you work through the items on and in your table, keep in mind this question: Is this useful? Then, throw out any clutter.

Decide on the purpose. Ask yourself: What is the function of this dresser? For example, if you lack wardrobe space, you can store your clothes here, Or it will hold items that you use every day. It's up to you.

A dresser is one of the best storage solutions for the living room, allowing you to simplify and enjoy the area you relax into the fullest.

Cut clutter in the living room closet

Is your closet in the living room jammed with stuff? If so, you are not alone. Luckily, with the right setup, you will find a place for every item. Take everything out of the closet. Work systematically around the entire space. Ready, set, go!

Create three piles:
1. Stuff that shouldn't go in the closet;
2. Items that should go in the cabinet;
3. Clutter and garbage.

Follow these few steps, and you will clean out your closet quickly and effortlessly. Then you should sort your items one by one.

Keep the clutter down by organizing all your necessities in a closet

- After decluttering, you should organize the living room closet according to your preferences. Ask yourself: What is the function of this closet?
- The living room is an area where the closet is a big help.

You can choose a tall narrow closet to maximize space.

- There are so many brilliant ideas to maximize closet space. Remember to use hangers with clips, multiple & tiered hangers, hooks, baskets, and other great solutions to keep your closet neat and tidy.

This versatile storage can hold all kinds of items, from your coats to yoga mats. If you still need more storage space, a console cabinet is a perfect solution for your essentials.

You get a lot of extra storage with hanging shelves

There are a lot of day to day necessities that make our living room look messy. Especially if we have kids. Are you wondering what to do with this pile of newspapers, books, toys, snacks and other items that are scattered all over your living room? How about you try using floating shelves?! Floating shelves are an inexpensive and practical solution for your living room. They are easy to install so you will get extra storage without taking up floor space. You can find them in attractive colors and different sizes to fit your living room. Good luck!

Floating shelves – decorative and functional ideas

Decorative and functional floating shelves can be mounted on nearly any wall in your living room. They offer you plenty of accessorizing options. These fabulous shelves can be grouped or stacked, so you will get extra storage and space to display your favorite possessions. Floating shelves cut clutter and add style to your living room at the same time.

Here's a practical idea to organize your houseplants.

Arrange your houseplants on floating shelves, offering you easy access for watering and upkeep, and providing an elegant and chic decorative detail. This way your living room will be both beautiful and functional!

Get the right coffee table

To get extra storage space in your living room, you can purchase a coffee table with built-in storage, either with open shelf storage or shelf drawers. Drawers can conceal all sorts of necessities such as remotes, books, magazines, and coasters, so you will be able to turn a simple table into a great storage facility.

Organize your coffee table

Is the coffee table surface jammed with clutter? Does anything belong in another room? Can anything be tossed out?

Your coffee table is perfect for items that are likely to be frequently used, but you need to make the most of your storage options. Clean your coffee table and clear surplus items out of drawers. Now you can use it for a stack of your favorite magazines, books you are reading, use coasters and candle holders, etc.

Dress up your coffee table

Take back control of the valuable surface of your coffee table with this simple hack. Place a beautiful tray, or some plates, on your table to corral small items. In this way, you will discourage putting all sorts of things on your coffee table because they already have their home.

Cute nesting tables – the solution for a small living room

This arrangement serves as a multi-tiered coffee table in your living room. It is an easy to move a piece of furniture, and it provides you with more possibilities than open coffee tables. These cute nesting tables are ideal for small living rooms because they take up less space.

Nesting tables come in sets of two or three, so you get an extra tabletop surface as needed.

Old-fashioned ottoman

This is an excellent storage furnishing because it can conceal a large number of items. The furniture comes in a variety of styles, designs, sizes, and colors so that you can bring order to your living room in a stylish way.

Remove the lid, and you can store anything from blankets to toys.

Built-Ins - maximize space in your living room

Built-ins will give your living room a well-organized appearance. You can frame your doorway with shelves and add fantastic storage to your living room. You can organize your books or display your favorite collection.

Built-ins can turn an unused space in the living room into a multi-functional storage. You can use irregularly shaped walls and nooks. Make the most of your small living room!

Just imagine – a storage bench!

Use your imagination and visualize two functions in one. Yes, it is a storage bench! It provides a place to sit, and space below can be used for bins. This is a real space saver. Corral kids' toys, craft supplies, and other trinkets and conceal them under your bench. You can choose from many designs and styles, and your living room will get a stylish and well-organized appearance.

Organize your favorites – collectible figurines

It's time to find the right home for your collectibles. Display them and add an artistic touch to your walls.

Floating shelves are a savvy solution for your favorite collectibles. In this way, you will get a stunning home décor that declutters and stores at the same time.

Rolling cart in your living room

The rolling cart is an especially good idea for a small living room.

If you need extra counter space, consider buying a vehicle.

A small rolling bar cart is just what you need to make things more manageable. And you can place your car anywhere you want. It can serve as a good home for your houseplants.

Tackle kids' belongings

If your children use the coffee table for board games and drawing, no big deal. Teach them to remove the supplies off the coffee table after each play session. Then, they should store their belongings in the place designated. Gather small items such as toy bricks and blocks, pencils and kids' craft supplies and conceal them. Nevertheless, as mentioned previously, the best solution is to set up desks or work tables for those activities. However, if you don't have a space for an additional piece of furniture, use stylish canvas storage bins and empty your living room. It is a great solution when you are in a hurry.

Living room organization – baskets

If you find you can't use your living room for what it was meant for, it's time to solve this problem. This is the area where the family can socialize with one another. Your living room is a perfect place for gatherings with family and friends, but not if it's jammed with stuff.

If you're living room is filled with knick-knacks, consider buying beautiful straw baskets. You can keep lots of different things in them. Remove clutter from your coffee table, armchairs, and floor. You can go one step further and purchase the baskets with handles to hang them on a wall using hooks.

Creative storage ideas for a small living room

After decluttering your home, you realize that there are lots of items of sentimental value to you! If you would like to save the items of great importance to you, you should find them a "home" in your "home." It could be your living room.

Install a small rectangular shelf for open storage, to display your favorites such as precious books, antiques and family heirlooms to best effect.

Creative organization solutions – freestanding cabinets

If you are looking for a stylish way to organize your home, consider installing freestanding cabinets. This amazing, versatile kind of furniture can be used to separate the living room from the rest of the house. It also provides you with a large amount of storage.

Burlap buckets as talented organizers

How about stylish burlap-covered buckets? You can use them to hold odds and ends, craft supplies, and other necessities. Then, hang them on the wall and get a clutter-free environment!

Apart from photographs and paintings, you can hang your favorite collections on the wall. You can also purchase a stylish ottoman with storage space and hide your burlap baskets there.

A single drawer file cabinet

A mini filing cabinet will not take a lot of space in your living room, but it is incredibly practical. It serves as a storage facility for your files and documents, as well as a side table. Use its surface to showcase your decorations or use it as a mini coffee table. It is a simple solution for concealing clutter when you are in a hurry. Your discreet cabinet still needs an occasional clean-up, so get rid of excess items from time to time.

Put furniture to work – console table

Multipurpose furniture is a must-have in your small living room. Choose furniture with moving parts and storage space, so you will save space and cut clutter at the same time. Consider buying a console table and add style to your living room. Trendy baskets can be lined up beneath for extra space storage.

Add glam to narrow shelves

Add style and glamour to your home with small shelves. They are perfect for easy access to the things you use every day in your living room. Remember – any unused space is a great spot for storage opportunities! Don't neglect the corners because they are the perfect place for those shelves. Small narrow shelves will provide you with just enough space for your everyday items, as well as beautiful display space for your collectibles.

Traditional hutches and armoires

Tackle the clutter problem with these old pieces of furniture.

Don't go out and shop for storage pieces before you sort through your living room. If you have an old armoire jammed with clutter, consider emptying and repairing it, and you will get a lot of extra space for storage.

Hutches and armoires provide you with plenty of concealed storage for organizing your items.

A simple hack – cute decorative trays

Opt for decorative trays to keep small items and necessities that you use on a daily basis organized. Find a "home" for your eyewear, small toys, pencils, books, craft projects, office supplies, etc. Here is a brilliant idea: each family member can be assigned a tray for holding everyday items.

Pro organizer trick – a table skirt

Here's an opportunity to express your creativity! Choose a stylish table skirt to hide your organization storage under the table. Corral your necessities and put them in the baskets. Then, hide your baskets behind the table skirt. So glam!

Organize your mini bar

For this purpose, you can find a metal cart with glass and bottle support. It is just what you need to make things a lot easier. When you're hosting a party, use your rolling cart. Only move the whole station all over your living room.

Bright ideas to make the most of the space in your living room

Your home entertainment center probably consists of the TV set, DVD/CD player, sound system, a collection of DVDs and CDs, etc. And all these items can create a disorganized jumble. You can save floor space by installing a flat panel, wall-mounted television. If you have an older TV set, tuck it into a tv cabinet or an armoire.

An armoire can also provide extra storage space in your living room. It is a very good idea for small apartments. So keep it in mind and think twice before getting rid of your old armoire.

Organize books according to your style

If you are a big fan of books, you can face the problem of too many books and a lack of shelves. Drawers won't shut, shelves are full and old books can be found in every room. Books, books, book... So you finally realize that it's time to let go of some of them.

The advice is simple – remove the excess and set yourself free!

There is no doubt, it is a large project, but it is important to start somewhere.

1. First of all, you must get rid of some books. What can you do with your old and unwanted books? You can sell these books online or donate them to the local library.
2. Now dust the shelves and the books. You can use a vacuum cleaner for some of the books.
3. Next logical step, sort your books by genre or author. You can also arrange them by their frequency of use. It's totally up to you. The books should be nicely and neatly sorted and easily accessible.
4. Keep in mind that you can store thousands of books on

your e-reader. Keep your books organized from now on; enjoy reading!

Cut the book clutter with stylish bookcases

Stylish furniture is one of the best ways to keep your books neatly organized. They are perfect for storing magazines, ornaments, family photographs, and other accessories.

You can go one step further and use bookends and magazine holders.

Use fabric-covered box files for storing day-to-day paperwork.

Prevent magazine clutter

Are your floor and tabletops cluttered with magazines? Are your magazines stacked in piles in the corner of your living room? It's time to cut that clutter once and for all!

1. Bring all your magazines together.
2. Have a trash bag on hand and toss unwanted magazines. Dispose of everything that you haven't used in the last year, and you will never use again. Try to recycle your magazines and do your part to keep the environment clean.
3. Decide which magazines you need to keep. If your thought is – "I probably should read this," get it out of your house. If you need to read magazines for a work assignment or your kids need some of them for school, you can keep them.
4. Sort and organize your magazines.

Keep your magazines neatly organized (Part I)

You love your magazines so much but do you have magazine holders? Or do you have a special home for them, for example, on a bookshelf? If your answer is No, it's time to sort your favorites. Here are a few ideas on how to do that quickly and effortlessly.

- A good solution is to purchase a couple of magazine racks.
- Go to your local store and pick a stylish magazine holder. Display your magazines in the living room and delight your guests who love to read magazines.
- A vertical spine bookcase is a very good idea if you have a huge collection of magazines; in this way, you can group them by category.

Enjoy your clutter-free living room!

Keep your magazines neatly organized (Part II)

There are a lot of extraordinary ways to sort your magazines.

- A stylish crate on wheels is a very good idea.
- Consider hanging decorative buckets and bins and find a perfect home for your favorite magazine collections. You can opt for over-the-door magazine storage pockets.
- You can use these ideas to organize all your ripped out magazine pages, too. Good luck!

Organize your comic book collection

- You should place your comics in protective bags to keep them safe from dirt and spills. These bags come in three most common materials: polyethylene, Mylar, and polypropylene.
- Then put your comics in the right boxes. Finding acid-free boxes is good. You could arrange them by series or by the publisher; it's up to you. Consider buying a comic notebook as a perfect solution for your favorites.
- After that, you should find a storage spot for your collectibles.

Make a better visual impression – hide electronics

Sometimes, even a few essential tech pieces can make clutter. For that reason, keeping your living room tidy and organized can be challenging. Especially if you own a small living space.

You can tuck your scanner or printer into a drawer and just take them out when needed.

Cubbies in your living room

Cubbies are an ideal furnishing for the living room. They are easy to manage and rearrange. Cubbies are great for storage and display. How to make the most of your cubby system? Follow a few simple steps.

- Take everything out and lay it on the ground. Throw out, donate or recycle everything that is useless.
- Wipe down your cubbies.
- Reorganize your items by categories. Use baskets if needed to keep everything neat and tidy. Organize your collectibles, photographs, figurines, books and other favorites.

Home office in your living room

You can set up your home office inside a closet in your living room. And you will get plenty of storage space. With the door closed, nobody knows your home office is there. This is one of the clever tricks of all time.

A great solution for extra storage in your living room

You can frame your sofa with custom cubbies that will provide you with extra storage space.

First and foremost, get rid of all unwanted items to free up space for necessities. Then, arrange your items, grouping them by categories.

You can install a mix of open and closed storage. In that way, you can display your favorites and hide some items. Make the most of your living room with this savvy design solution!

6. Children's Room

Declutter kids' rooms – well begun is half done!

While the same ground rules for cleaning up apply when you organize the children's room, there are some small differences and additional considerations. How to begin?

- First and foremost, you should involve your kids in the process of cleaning their rooms. The primary and the most important goal is to teach them how to care for their things.
- Before you start cleaning, sit down and try to explain the organization process to them. They should understand the basics, so stick to simplicity. Everything else will be described during the process.
- Make space for children's questions. If children understand what is expected of them, they will be much more cooperative.

Let's play the "Cut clutter game"!

This is a unique challenge for you and your kids. After explaining the cleaning process, it's time to go from intention to realization. Here is a step-by-step guide:

- Toss and put away: Use trash and recycle boxes or bags. Toss every toy that is missing important parts or is broken. You should decide on this together with your kids. You can create a "not sure" box but decide as soon as possible.
- Cleaning: Use this opportunity to dust, vacuum and wipe down furniture. It's a good idea to involve your

kids in cleaning their room.

- Divide and conquer: To achieve the best results, you can split the children's room into several central zones. These are 1) the sleeping zone, 2) the study area, 3) the entertaining area, and 4) the grooming area.

Declutter kid's room – surplus furniture

If a child's room is jammed with surplus furniture, it's time to make things cleaner. Having too many tables, baskets, etc. make the rooms appear smaller.

- Get rid of surplus furniture. Consider what will stay and what will go. You can sell them at a garage sale, or you can donate them. The same basic rule for decluttering applies here – less is more!
- The way you arrange furniture can make a big difference. Find an appealing spot for every piece.

How to declutter the children's bedroom?

Toss it or keep it. While you are going through the room, ask yourself: "Do my kids need all these things in the room?" and "Is anything in their sleeping area unused?" Remember to ask: "What's important to my child?" Then, toss unwanted items.

Sort all the items lying around. Designating a spot for each and every item is important. Put things back in their places.

Buy organizing products by considering the bigger picture.

After dividing the kid's room into zones, you have to set up individual spots for certain items. What to do next? Of course, you should buy organizers. You can also make them yourself. Just make sure to purchase organizers that match the décor of the kids' room. Considering the aesthetics is important. If you have no idea what to buy and find this difficult, stick to a well-known rule – The simpler, the better!

Organize a comfortable sleeping area.

It's so easy to let a child's room become chaotic; moreover, most people have a small child's bedroom. It's important to clean up under bed space periodically.

- Pick all the rubbish off the floor and throw it away. Remove all items that don't belong in the kids' bedroom.
- You should only have pillows and one soft toy on the child's bed.
- Then, make a bedside table. Free up space for necessities such as a glass of water, a lamp, and maybe a magazine or a book. Consider buying a bedside table with drawers so your child will be able to put necessities out of sight. In this way, you will keep it from getting too messy.

Maintain the kids' room

To maintain your fresh and uncluttered environment, stick to a few ground rules:

- Make beds every morning.
- Keep kids' clothing organized. Place it in the closet or the laundry basket.
- Take control of bedside clutter. Make sure kids don't ruin what you have achieved.

Organize the kids' study space

Tired of messy kids' desks? By cleaning and organizing the kids' study space, you'll feel less stressed, and your house will be well organized.

You will need two basic things: a child-friendly desk, a storage space for school and craft supplies.

1. Kid's desk serves as a homework station, as well as a work area. Therefore, make sure they have a good-sized and uncluttered work surface. Throw away everything that is useless. Divide into sections to make cleaning easier. For example, clean up and sort items in only one drawer. Do not go on until you have finished that job. Then, choose another drawer or shelf, and so on. Rome wasn't built in a day!

2. The storage solution is a significant issue for your overall organization. So, make sure to provide your kids with enough storage space. Choose from different drawers, cabinets, baskets, bins and other storage solutions according to your needs. This makes it easier for kids to find their possessions.

Use desktop and drawer organizers

Is your kids' desk cluttered with papers, pens, rulers, notebooks and other items? Do you want to help your children bring order to their homework station? The solution is simple – use desktop and drawer organizers. Your children can divide their items and group them into categories for better organization results. Choose from different designs, patterns, and sizes and create an excellent space for studying and creative activities.

7. Garden, and Backyard

If you are someone who has a patio, garden or backyard then you do need to clean it often. Take out time during the weekend and consider cleaning it properly. Since it is the free side of your house, it will be dirtier than the indoor room. You can clean your crazy backyard with easy tips in good weather. Make sure it is not so warm when you are cleaning it because then it can be bad for your health. Prefer to do it during the evening before the sunset so that you can see and the weather also settles by that time whether it is winters or summers season. Here are some of the tips which you can follow to clean the patio, garden, and the backyard.

Stay Prepared

Plan in the mind what you want to clean such as the whole area or some part of the area for now. Then have the right tools for it to clean because you will be cutting off the big branches and the grass as well as picking up trash which is there from unknown places. You need to have the right supplies to get started once so that you do not end up wasting your time while searching for one again and again. Be prepared and then step outdoor to clean it.

Get Started

A lot of people get confused when trying to figure out which area should be cleaned first. You can start with removing trash from the messiest areas and then move towards the areas that are not so messy; this way, you will not get tired before you are done.

Get the Family Involved

You can engage your children in cleaning activities, and you will be surprised about how happy they will be happy to help you. If you are on one side, they can help you bring in the supply which you need from the other corner. The kids will be able to learn something new while you will get the cleaning done within the shortest time possible.

Feed the Plants

When taking care of the plants in your garden or backyard, it is of prime importance that you look out for plants with stunted growth. If any, you ought to trim or cut them down or else they will decay and cause problems for other neighboring plants. For this reason, be sure to water, fertilize and prune your plants.

Hire a Gardener

If you are too busy and do not have time at all to get the cleaning done in these areas, and they prefer to hire a gardener. A professional gardener will know the best what they need to do and how they can take care of the area. They do not just look after the plants but also make sure to clean the area so that the environment stays clean. Ask your friends and relatives to recommend someone reliable who can work on your garden to keep it maintained and look better all the time. If you can afford it then definitely go for this choice.

Principle 4: How to maintain order?

Living frugally and without debt is a lifestyle, and it may take some time for you to get used to it, but it is so freeing that it is worth all of the work that goes into it. When you decide that you want to live frugally and without debt, sit down and make a list of reasons why you want to do so.

Keep this list of reasons close by so that if you start to feel like you are missing out on certain things in life, you will be reminded of what your goals are. One of the rules in our house is that if we don't have a coupon for it, we do not purchase it. So, if you want something, search the internet for a coupon for it or just wait until it goes on sale.

Another part of living the frugal lifestyle is taking care of the things you have and respecting what you have spent your money on. So what if you own a $50 couch, that is $50 out of your pocket, take care of it and respect it.

I want to talk to you about passing on the frugal lifestyle. How great would it feel if you could say your children would never be in debt? What about if you knew that they would never go without or want because you taught them how to save and spend money wisely. If for no other reason than this, I hope that you take the tips in this book and implement them into your life.

Before making the decision to start living frugally, you must understand that saving on cash requires you to be committed. You will be required to give up some conveniences, and trust me if you follow through with this in a few months you won't even miss them.

Now, how are you going to implement these changes? As I mentioned earlier, I want you to pick a few of the tips I have given you and start making those changes in your life. Let it be a gradual process; apply some changes this week and apply some more changes the following week.

You don't want to make too many changes at once because if you do, you will find that they are harder to stick to. Most people want to make huge changes in their lives, and they fail because they are asking too much of themselves. But if you add in small changes, you will barely notice them, and you will raise your chances of being successful.

There are moments you will backslide and not act as planned. For instance, you are going to see something in the store that you like and buy it on impulse or order something off of the internet, but when this happens don't give up, keep your head up and start again.

We as humans only learn through failure and if you fail along the way, take note of it then move on. This only gets easier as time goes on.

The Making of a Budget

In a society where money has little or no meaning,People tend to spend too much money buying anything they set their eyes on. If you keep doing this on a daily basis, at the end of the month you will be broke, and not able to pay your bills. However, if you think through your purchases before initiating them, then you might have avoided the problem in the first place. So, how do people make sure that they have all the money they need to not stress at the end of a month?

The answer to this is a budget. Having one of these handy tools at your fingertips can influence how and where you spend your money on a daily basis. The sad part of the matter is that not many people understand or know how to budget their money to achieve financial success. It's my goal to help you figure out what makes up a budget and how using one can drastically improve your financial situation and cash flow.

So, let's start at the beginning and analyze what a budget is and how to build one to suit your personal needs. Once you have a firm understanding of budgeting, you will be able to make your own budget and see the benefits it can bring in your life.

A budget is essentially a tool that shows you where your money goes and where your money comes from. It then takes your income and subtracts your expenses from it, showing you if you have money left at the end of the month, or if you are going to be short on funds. Once you have all of your bills plugged into this budget, you can see where your money goes and where changes need to be made to ensure that you do have money left at the end of the month.

Building a budget is quite simple, and your computer's office documents should have templates to help you make your budget.

These spreadsheets will calculate your findings for you, taking the guesswork out of the process. If you have the resource, try plugging in your expenses and income and see what it tells you.

One thing that you need to keep in mind when building a budget is the miscellaneous money you spend that you might not even realize is leaving your hand. Think about when you stop to grab a cup of coffee or soda. These transactions do affect your budget, even though they seem petty and small. Adding the two to three dollars you spent at the coffee shop could influence your budget if you do it repeatedly.

Therefore, when building a budget, include every time you spend money or make money. Every penny can affect your overall financial situation, even if it seems like a small and unworthy transaction. If it helps, try looking at your bank statements and see where you used your card or withdrew money from the ATM. These all add up to the and just a few dollars could make a huge difference when you need to pay that power bill at the end of the month!

Are you ready to build your budget? Then round up your receipts and bills, and let's see where your money is going. If it's a shock to you, then it may be a very good time to change your spending habits to be able to save money and see an active figure at the end of the month.

In the following chapters, I'm going to give you some tips and advice on ways you can use to ensure that you spend less money so that you can have a positive-looking budget. I'm also going to show you some creative ways you can use to ensure that you spend less on geeds and services you purchase on a daily basis. Ready?

Principle 5: Maybe you should hire a cleaner?

Enlisting proficient cleaners is, definitely, a keen move. The motivation behind this statement can be summed up with four words: time, productivity, quality, and certification. The estimation of astounding cleaning administrations is more than what it costs when you consider the upsides of having residential cleaners deal with your home.

Time is the one thing that runs so fast that we even lose track of it sometimes. For this reason, leisure time is treasured. Such spared time can be spent doing different things that those day by day schedules and timetables leave little time for. With regards to local cleaning, there are individuals that are gifted in administrations and can easily do a thorough cleaning job for you; at a wallet-friendly price. These individuals come equipped with all the necessary stuff for cleaning; so, do not waste much time trying to figure out which cleanser, brush or synthetic cleans every area of your house. Alternatively, you can go take care of other pressing issues as you leave the cleaning job to the experts

The effectiveness of cleaning organizations is confirmed by the way they complete the administrations. Their administrations are classified into the different parts of the home. They incorporate yet aren't restricted to cover tidying and cleaning, floor waxing, blind washing, broiler cleaning, clothing, pressing, cultivating et cetera. A mortgage holder can select a booked cleaning administration for each of the different viewpoints. One is guaranteed that each specific part will get singular consideration and verification that viable cleaning is accomplished. The absence if other peoples input is a substantially more astute way to deal with home cleaning than choosing to do all the work yourself.

The nature of the consequences of expert residential cleaning is measured by its result. Great quality is accomplished by gifted people, and as hard as it is for anybody to be an ace of all exchanges, an individual can't take in everything that is involved in a complete home cleaning. Cleaning organizations typically have a differing cleaning group. Each is spent significant time in a specific field of cleaning, and subsequently, quality cleaning work falls into place without any issues.

Having an assurance that you're cleaning needs will be met, regardless of whether you are available amid the procedure or not, will give you a significant serenity that is invaluable. It's the administrators' unadulterated virtuoso that gives you more comfort. At the point when a house keeping organization is contracted and a timetable set, it now turns into the obligation of the business to guarantee that all the fundamental cleaning is done precisely and on time. This it needs to do, as an issue of legally binding commitments as well as a feature of its self-protection. Presently with such a confirmation, a man is allowed to unwind in the solace that his or her home will dependably be perfect. Such a tranquil sort of living is definitely, a keen move.

Currently, men and ladies lead confounded and occupied lives. They are often excessively occupied with, making it impossible to manage ordinary assignments, for example, cleaning the house. However, does that imply that they have to live in a pig pen? Obviously not! Individuals in this circumstance can procure Domestic Cleaners.

What are Home Cleaners?

Local Cleaners are individuals who function as house keepers in the home. They visit a customer's home amid planned circumstances and clean the house. Recorded underneath are a portion of the errands that these cleaners can deal with.

- Cleaning general mess and wreckage around the home
- Putting things back in their standard area
- Vacuuming and cleaning the floors
- Wiping down windows and other dusty surfaces
- Washing dishes
- Cleaning the lavatory and the latrine
- Laundry related administrations, for example, washing, drying and collapsing garments
- Cleaning up after creatures and little youngsters.

Step by step instructions to locate a decent private more clean

As there are a few cleaners out there, customers need to figure out how to separate a decent channel from a normal specialist. Customers should search for the accompanying qualities in a cleaning organization.

- Reputation. Organizations with great notorieties have them for one reason - their past clients have been satisfied with the administrations they gave. For this situation, a great notoriety implies that the cleaning organization is moderate, legitimate and equipped.

-   An organization that contracts experienced staff. Individuals frequently wrongly think that anyone can clean house. This is not genuine with regards to proficient cleaning. Dynamic cleaners will be physically fit and ready to deal with high cleaning arrangements securely.

-   Pricing. When 'shopping' for cleaning administrators, you look out for those that offer good services at a pocket-friendly price. Administrators have different charges for different services; so be sure that you have the money to pay for a service before hiring. Get yourself a magnificent administration that fits inside their financial plan.

Does employing a cleaner mean you are languid?

Individuals are frequently hesitant to procure a cleaner since they are anxious about the possibility of being perceived to be lethargic. In the event that this is a worry, purchasers should consider how much their chance is worth.

For instance, a parent who spends the end of the week cleaning could procure a cleaner and go through the day with their tyke. Quality time with the family is extremely valuable and procuring a cleaner can make it conceivable.

Also, enabling cleaners to deal with employments around the home lessens feelings of anxiety. Clients will never again need to stress over all the work they should return to by the day's end.

On the off chance that a shopper needs additional administrations, they should check whether the organization offers that administration. A few organizations additionally offer childcare and senior care administrations.

Procuring a household cleaner can free up a customer's psyche and give them an opportunity to do the things they cherish. Cleaning the house ought not to be a need as it comprises of humble undertakings which should be done routinely. Rather, clients can utilize their opportunity to improve their work/family or social lives.

The procuring of residential cleaners has been training among the overall population for a long time. These experts are an indispensable piece of our general public and thousands are contracted each year in a wide range of regions of the capital. You may need to hire the services of a residential cleaner if you can't finish the cleaning activity yourself either because of physical conditions or inadequate time amid the day. These services come in handy to many people as people have unlimited errands to run causing them to have little or no time to thoroughly clean the house.

When concentrating on the cleanliness of your home, it without a shadow of a doubt can be an endless assignment, particularly on the off chance that you work for extend periods of time or you happen to be a solitary parent or even both! There can be some super residential cleaners accessible to mortgage holders on a day by day, week after week, month to month or even an irregular premise. They can be reserved through cleaning organizations that can redo your cleaning administrations to oblige your each need.

You may just need a specific range of your home cleaned like a family room or kitchen after a substantial get-together, yet regardless of the measure of the activity, household cleaners are accessible to help you.

The cost to clean your house is generally in view of a few components; How dirty your house is and the number of times you hire the services of a local cleaner can determine how much you are charged. .. The sort of local cleaning can likewise factor into the cost. For instance, if a property holder has pets in their home this might be an occupation that would take additional time as extra insurances should be chosen to tidy up a dirty cover or dander on furniture. Surfaces that require particular cleaning may likewise take additional time and in this manner will cost more cash.

When you initially choose to hire the services of a cleaning organization, you might need to ensure that they have a safety guarantee such that they completely check their representatives previously doling out them to any properties. Immediately you have chosen someone you can trust to do the cleaning for you; it is of essence to have them come to your home so that you can show them their way around the house particularly the areas you need cleaned.

By hiring household cleaners, you will have the capacity to give yourself less things to stress over in the home and will have the capacity to give significantly greater quality time with your family or to just unwind before the TV without looking over at a heap of grimy dishes or a smudged cover.

Principle 6: What did we miss?

Hobby

Being frugal does not mean that you are not going to be able to have any fun. Yes, you are going to have to spend some extra time cooking your meals at home and working on DIY projects, but you don't have to live a life without any fun just because you want to be frugal. There are plenty of ways to enjoy life and live frugal at the same time.

One of the things my family loves to do is swim. We tend to do this on a daily basis when the weather allows, but we are not willing to pay $3 per person per day to swim at the pool. Instead, we take off down to the river and spend a few hours splashing around. There are fewer people there and if too many people show up all we have to do is move upstream just a bit. There is always enough room for us at the river. You can also go to the beach or a lake depending on the water body in your area. Make sure if you are going to be there for very long you pack some extra food, so the kids are not screaming to grab fast food on the way home.

Speaking of packing some extra food, picnics are a great way to spend time with your family and not spend any extra money. One thing my kids love to do in the summer is making a picnic lunch and sit out in the yard and eat it. You don't have to go very far, just going outside to eat is a ton of fun for kids. You can also have a night where you cook hotdogs and smores over a fire. This is an excellent way to relax and spend some time getting some fresh air.

Camping was always something that we loved to do when we were kids and still love to do to this day. Pack up the family and spend a few days camping out in the woods. Find an area that does not charge a fee and is close to a river. Have the kids fish for their dinner and save even more. (Always make sure you bring some backup food just in case they don't catch anything.)

Take up a hobby that is both fun and saves you money. One thing that my children and I love to do is clip coupons. This is my hobby, but it is also a way that we can spend time together as a family. You can also go for walks, or exercise together as a family;get healthy and enjoy nature all at the same time.

Get your family involved in some DIY projects. Kids love to help plant a garden and care for it. They love to plant flowers and care for them as well. Get them involved in any project that you are working on and it will not only be fun for them, but it will also be a great memory that lasts a lifetime. I guarantee it will mean more to them than the time you took them to an amusement park and spent $300.

Just because you are living a frugal lifestyle does not mean that you have to be boring. Some of the most interesting people I know live a frugal way of life. They are always doing something, working on some project or having fun with their families. They are happier than those I know who do not live a frugal lifestyle.

Garage

The garage is a great rec room, workshop or hobby area if you manage to keep it clean; as you may have noticed over the years, many innovations and inventions have originated in the garages of people. Here are some quick hacks that will help you clean your garage.

First off, avoid using your garage as a storeroom or dumping ground. Store only things you need and find a way to get rid of the rest, which just makes the area stay organized. A lot of random and unnecessary stuff is only going to add to the chaos and should be taken care of immediately.

Organize your things properly in boxes. Label them and stack them in an organized manner to promote maximum productivity. Labeling and stacking not only improve productivity but also make sure that things are convenient to reach and find in case of emergencies. In an unmaintained garage, you might end up looking for something for more than a few minutes.

Install wall hooks and hang your tools there. This makes it much easier to access them, and it looks neat as well. Wall hooks can be done from old cup holders or coat hangers. By hanging your tools up you not only increase the aesthetics of the place but also the productivity.

Clean and oil your tools from time to time to prevent them from rusting. Use a mixture of vinegar and rust solution and make a paste. Leave it overnight and rub it off using an old toothbrush. This technique may not be able to remove all the stains at once. However, it will work in the long run.

Oil stains on garage floors can be removed using blotting paper. Just place the blotting paper over the area and run an iron over it. The dye will stick to the paper when you pull it off. The residual stain can be removed by wiping that area with a mixture of lemon juice and rubbing alcohol.

Spray a mixture of water and any essential oil you like to keep your garage smelling fresh like the rest of your house.

Mop the floor with rubbing alcohol, lemon juice and essential oil mixed with water. This will clean the area and leave a pleasant smell behind as well.

Put up shelves along the walls using day-to-day materials. This improves the level of storage and therefore productivity. It also improves ease of cleaning and reduces the effort required.

For those people who have a small garage, you might always be worried about nicking the door of your car against the wall. For such cases, line the walls of the garage with foam strips or thick sponge. This will act as a cushion and control the amount of damage done.

A garage is bound to have storage of a lot of small things like nails, screws, *etc.* It is particularly annoying when someone knocks over the whole thing. An easy hack to this would be to conceal a magnet behind the bowls. This attraction will make sure that all the pins are in the same box and will make accidents easier to clean up after.

Animal in the house

"Pets are such pleasing companions, they pose no inquiries, and they pass no reactions," said George Eliot in regards to pet creatures. Pets regularly respond to the adoration that their lords shower on them by showing different types of friendship including licking, hickeys, even love-nibbles. Most people nowadays rear animals because of the benefits an animal bring to them. For example, one will rear chickens because then will get eggs from them. This goes without saying; if you want free eggs, then you may have to raise your own chickens. However, many people have trouble eating the chickens that they raise; if you are one of these people, just get enough chickens to produce the number of eggs you need each day! If you have extra eggs, you can always sell them. In the summer, you can allow your chickens to roam around your yard and eat up all the bugs along with some grass to cut back on chicken feed.

There's no other activity that can be compared to keeping a pet. Pet care is, truth be told, a stable situation, and incorporates the fundamental elements of prepping and endeavoring to keep up great pet social insurance. General pet supplies could be viewed as a meaning of helpful devices for prepping and keeping your pet healthy.

Pet Supplies:

A fundamental rundown of pet supplies for buy could incorporate the accompanying: pet sustenance and nourishment dishes, pet id labels and collars, pet meds, supplements, and tonics, and so on. Some different things to consider are creature bearers, pet houses and furniture, pet beds, garments, and pet adornments.

Pet Grooming Supplies:

Pet prepping supplies incorporate things, for example, preparing scissors, pet hair mind items, cleansers, cleanser, and aromas.

Pet Health Care:

Pet social insurance is a fundamental obligation of pet proprietorship. For puppies and little cats, or some other four-legged pets, essential medications would incorporate giving a cleanliness shower, cleaning, brushing, brushing, checking cars, paws, teeth and underside of the tongue, nail trimming, evacuating bugs and creepy crawlies, and settling customary gatherings with an expert veterinary. A decent pet proprietor ought to take after a general timetable of preparing sessions.

Pet care can require a great deal of tolerance. Like kids, pets regularly require uncommon consideration. A puppy, little cat or some other pet in its outset should be taken care of with extraordinary care. Specifically, they should be propped legitimately, bolstered deliberately, and had relations with appropriately.

Pet Grooming

The pet preparing business is a prospering business today. There are various pet preparing schools offering the comparable administrations of a pet prepping proficient. Individuals enlist the administrations of these expert specialists for the best possible prepping of their pets. Proficient pet prepping is ending up very well known in United States, Canada, and European nations.

Most pet proprietors consider their four-legged companions as individuals from the family. Proprietors recount clever stories to companions about their pets entertaining tricks. Some pet proprietors even praise the birthday celebrations of their catlike and canine allies. Like other relatives, proprietors nestle with pets, converse with them, nurture them when they are wiped out, and rebuff them when they do things that are against the tenets. While most pets are very much acted, numerous proprietors have returned home to discover things torn to shreds by their puppy or that their feline dirtied a most loved sofa-bed. As much as proprietors may respond cruelly by hollering at or generally rebuffing their fuzzy companions consider the probability that these pets are carrying on of weariness, dejection, and division tension.

Actually many pets are liable to fatigue, forlornness and division nervousness similarly as kids seem to be. Despite the fact that it's difficult to defend the decimation of property, pet proprietors ought to be mindful so as not to humanize (to attribute human qualities to things not human) pet conduct. It is fundamental to understand that creatures require mental and physical incitement to forestall fatigue and dejection. Pets appreciate the organization of their kindred pack creatures to mitigate depression, for instance, and proprietor's tolerant and empathetic help in beating division uneasiness is basic.

Leave your pet for short periods of time and over time increase to longer periods. Leave the house when you do this exercise, as some pets are not easily fooled. When crate training a dog, use the same process. Abandon the dog in the crate for short periods of time, gradually building up to longer stretches. Contrary to what some pet owners believe, crates are not cruel devices for dogs. Dogs are den animals. They often prefer the security of feeling like they are in a warm, safe den-like enclosure. Many dogs that have been crate trained are often found relaxing in their wired den with the door open, happily chewing on a bone or taking a nap. Remember, however, that you should never use the crate as a form of punishment. The crate is a haven for your dog, not a time-out room and should always retain positive associations. Additionally, upon returning to home or upon removing a pet from the crate, owners should ignore their pet for a short while. Remember, your coming and going is not a big deal. The idea is that there is no cause for alarm or excitement when you depart or arrive.

In extreme cases of separation anxiety, the process of desensitizing a pet will need to be undertaken in minimal steps. Using a variation of the method described above, owners of an anxious pet must approach the desensitizing procedure carefully. Approach your morning routine as you normally would, but in small steps that easy understand.

Laundry

There is nothing more demoralizing than an untidy pantry. Consolidating the wreckage is an awesome advance to making it a lovelier errand.

In any case, clothing is an unpleasant activity. After only one wearing, clothing is ideal back in the hamper holding up to be washed once more. On the off chance that you can make the washing condition slightly additionally engaging, you will think that it's to a lesser extent an errand. The mystery is conveying some request to the pantry.

Make more space

The main trap is to influence more space in the clothing to room. This implies you have to improve utilization of the unused spaces. For instance, most pantries can exploit the space between the washer and the dryer. With as meager as 8 inches, you can include an arrangement of limited wicker drawers that fit between the washer and dryer. These four graduated drawers hold cleansing agent sheets, recolor sticks, and even your eyeglasses so you can read the labels on attire. The plastic front takes after hand-woven wicker. It quantifies 36 inches high, 19 inches profound and 8 inches wide.

With pretty much a similar measure of room, you can include a takeoff clothing caddy that stores some taller things, similar to clothing cleanser, cleanser, and the iron. The durable melamine caddy has three open racks with raised side rails to keep the items set up. The caddy is determined to double track casters, so it rapidly takes off and backpedals in the middle of the dryer and washer. It gauges 31 inches high, 25 inches profound and 8 3/8 inches wide. Some gathering is required.

Hanging traps

Here and there the most ideal approach to dispose of jumble is to go up. The overlap down over door clothing holder gives you a wardrobe where there is not one. It makes a place to hang garments when it leaves the dryer or if the clothing guidelines suggest line drying. It is made with a locking pivot that backings ten holders. At the point when it's not being used, simply overlap it down any way. At this point, you can feel a cushioning within the section so it won't begin to expose what's underneath and it fits over general entryways.

A simple approach to air dry your clothing is an arrangement of five hanging cuts. Made to fit over a towel bar or wire racking, these trickle dry hanging clothes pins let you air dry anything from the delicate to towels to socks. Their no-slip teeth keep your garments hung up and off the floor.

Clothing Carts

On the off chance that you have ever observed the clothing trucks in a Laundromat and figured they would be valuable at home, you are in good fortune. Clothing trucks are accessible in everything from business size to individual head servant estimate.

The clothing steward is sufficiently reduced to fit in the littlest pantries. The chrome plated steel outline has 3-inch mechanical wheels with twofold bolts and a vast wicker bin to hold your clothing. You can hang wet or dry pieces of clothing on the valet bar that ascent over the bushel. There is a base retire underneath the wicker container that can store clothing cleanser and different supplies. It quantifies 67½ inches high, 24½ inches wide and more than 20 inches thick.

In the event that you are searching for something with more storage room, consider the great antique bronze clothing focus with its three substantial obligations, removable canvas clothing packs. It likewise accompanies two packs - one for undergarments and one for sweaters. Hanging over the three clothing sacks is where you can hang the garments you simply pressed. There is additionally a high retire for putting away clean garments or clothing frill. The clothing focus will move over your home on smooth moving casters with two locking wheels. The bronze complete on the steel outline is sufficiently appealing you won't have any desire to hurry to put it away. It gauges 72 inches high, 30 inches wide and 18 inches thick.

Additional space

In the event that counter space is at a premium in your pantry, at that point you most likely could utilize some additional space where you can overlap your clothing. This steel, moving clothing station offers additional space and that's only the tip of the iceberg. The truck's two racks hold cleanser, cleanser, collapsed apparel and that's only the tip of the iceberg. There is a slide-out wire wicker bin that can hold little things, similar to recolor sticks, garments sticks and scissors to cut free strings. Whenever shut, the melamine entryways on top can be utilized to overlap clothing. They open to uncover a removable canvas sack. This moves along on casters and measures 31 inches high, 26¼ inches wide and 18 inches profound.

Another simple approach to build space is with a wire retire that mounts over the highest point of a washer or dryer. Measuring 26½ inches in length and 10 inches wide, the vinyl covered rack will effectively hold cleanser bottles and boxes.

Ashing and drying garments is one of the most established local errands. Before vacuum cleaners, dishwashers, stovetops or running water came into existence, individuals still needed to do the clothing. Garments was washed and cleaned in waterways, lakes and streams, and after that dried in the sun. The procedure was a throughout the day issue, even after the appearance of cleanser and the washboard. Things are somewhat less demanding today. Automated cleaning gadgets like the clothes washer and the garments dryer wound up plainly moderate in America toward the finish of the twentieth century. Yet, the procedure still requires some investment. After gathering, arranging, washing, drying and collapsing, the wash cycle eats up about two hours every day. We also accomplish more clothing than any other time in recent memory.

For clear reasons, the wash was ordinarily a week after week errand before the washer and dryer went ahead the scene. Presently it is an everyday undertaking. Truth be told, it is more than day by day. The normal family does four hundred heaps of wash every year. Despite the fact that the procedure will most likely never be agreeable, a few devices and adornments can, in any event, make it tolerable.

Pantry Organizers

The pantry is ordinarily the most jumbled and complicated room in the home. Some portion of the issue is that there is at times enough space. Oddly enough, engineers seldom pay much personality to the pantry, despite the fact that it is a standout amongst the most prevalent rooms in the home. Therefore, the room is regularly undersized for the work for which it was planned. This powers numerous mortgage holders to abhor the procedure considerably more than they ordinarily would. For, is the task unappealing, as well as the earth is lacking. Clothing coordinators can settle a significant number of these basic stockpiling issues.

Hampers

Before you do the wash, you should obviously gather the filthy garments. Hampers are a standout amongst the most conventional home coordinators since they can be set in like manner ranges. Dissimilar to the standard plastic clothing wicker bin, the hamper is ordinarily found outside of the pantry in corridors and rooms. There are additionally a wide range of sorts of wicker container that perform more than one capacity. There are flip-top hampers, falling hampers, moving wicker bin, hanging hampers and that's just the beginning.

Since most families have two guardians that work nowadays, the clothing frequently gets pushed to the end of the week. Doing seven or eight heaps of clothing on Saturday and Sunday has turned into another American convention. In any case, what do you do with all the grimy garments? A few people simply abandon them on the pantry floor, which is muddled as well as unsanitary. We like the rollout hamper for the pantry. These vast wicker bins are frequently introduced as drawers that straightforwardly sending when required.

For those that need additional hierarchical highlights, we prescribe the triple clothing sorter. These hampers have three separate compartments for whites, hues and blended garments, which dispenses with the need to sort or separate apparel before you do a heap of clothing. At the point when utilized outside of the pantry, it is regularly a smart thought to put marks on every compartment to tell relatives which garments to store in them.

For clear reasons, hampers that are put in the general population zones are significantly more upscale than those that are consigned to the pantry. The new bushel is made of alluring materials like canvas, wicker, and sea grass. They look simply like some other utilitarian bit of contemporary furniture.

Clothing Center

Most mortgage holders worship gadgets that perform more than one assignment. It makes their lives a considerable measure simpler. The clothing focus is presumably the most adaptable coordinator available today. Regularly found in inns and motels, it comes outfitted with a clothing sorter, a bar for hanging cleaning and a best retire for towels and bedding. Since it takes up a ton of room, the clothing focus is best for homes that have substantial pantries on the primary floor. The gadget may act as a burden in littler rooms, which clearly overcomes its motivation.

Clothing Caddy

As little as they frequently may be, numerous families utilize the pantry to store additional sustenance, which implies that rack and bureau space will be much harder to stop by. Pantry cleaners like dye, cleansers and stain removers regularly must be full into any open space or basically left on the floor. One clear and reasonable answer for this stockpiling issue is the clothing caddy. This little coordinator fits cozily between the washer and the dryer and makes utilization of beforehand unused space. The vast majority of the models we surveyed were furnished with three little retires that were, in any case, sufficiently huge to hold containers of blanch, cleansing agents, and cleansers. The clothing caddy has little casters that enable it to take off easily when required.

Principle 7: Cleaning plan

What do people mean by getting organized? Well, it means different things to different people. It could mean time management to some and know what's for dinner every night for somebody else. Or it could mean that your house is always neat and tidy.

A good way to achieve the latter is by setting up a cleaning schedule.

Cleaning the whole house top to bottom every day is neither desirable nor possible for most people due to work and other commitments. It is also not necessary. Different jobs need to be done at various intervals, and you need to find out what works for you, depending on how clean you want/need your house to be.

Here are three steps for setting up a cleaning schedule:

Step 1: List all the jobs you need/want to do around the house with their frequency. For instance: daily - washing dishes, cleaning the toilet, tidy up, take out trash; weekly - vacuuming, dusting; monthly - clean light fixtures, clean windows. These are just suggestions; your idea of a clean house might look differently.

Step 2: Divide the jobs up among all family members, children doing age-appropriate tasks. You can give people permanent employment or work on a Rota basis.

Step 3: Decide for the daily jobs when they ought to be done (before leaving the house in the morning or after returning home from work or school). The weekly jobs need a regular day, such as vacuuming every Monday, dusting every Friday. And the monthly jobs need also need to be slotted in on a particular weekday, such as clean light fixtures on Tuesday, alternating rooms every week so that all rooms get done once a month. This sounds more complicated than it is, once you create a plan on paper, it all becomes quite clear.

If you're not too sure what to include and how often you should be cleaning and tidying what, why not Google "household cleaning schedule" and see what other people have written on the subject. You'll even find fully fledged cleaning programs ready to print out and use.

There are also age appropriate chores lists if you have children and want to include them in fun. And yes, it can be fun. If you have a tick list to follow, and maybe even a treat in store for you once you finished all the items on your list, then you can make the whole thing into a game for yourself and your family. You might even race to see who finishes their jobs first and best and give out a little prize for the winner.

Daily

Before we even acknowledge we have to clean, we need to perceive something is grimy. We see or feel the earth and grime, and we know we have put off cleaning sufficiently long. We can look and know, in only a look, what we have to clean. When we put off cleaning these things, soil and grime start to develop, and we aren't as agreeable in them as we used to be.

There are a few things we put off cleaning since they are so grimy we would prefer not to experience the inconvenience of investing heaps of energy cleaning them. To in reality clean something, we need to have every one of the devices expected to take care of business right. We have to accumulate what we require before cleaning, chip away at taking care of business and after that influence a propensity for standard support to keep it to clean.

Our hearts and brains require a normal upkeep process which intends to helps us unwind after a long day. Without general cleaning in our souls and psyches, the fiend can come in and do his work. He blossoms in grimy house where he engages you in grimy considerations He goes ahead to make his insidious arrangements work when our psyches are jumbled up and not concentrated on God.

To begin with, we need to perceive that our hearts and brains are grimy. We need to comprehend what has been developing and what has made us end up noticeably unclean. It now and again gets dirty and the development shields us from seeing what the main problem is. That is the reason we require God to do our everyday cleaning. We have to give Him our earth and grime. We can't-do this cleaning without anyone else.

To plan to clean, we need to have the correct instruments. Cleaning requires an option that is other than our hands. We need to have clothes or fabrics. We need to have water or some cleaning fluid or powder. We need to have vitality and inspiration. To clean our psyches, we need to have God's instruments. We have to put on His covering. We have to peruse His pledge. We have to go to Him in the great circumstances and terrible.

Now and again, something is so filthy when we start the initial couple of rubs don't dispose of the earth and grime. We keep scouring without end the layers of tidy until the point when we see a perfect surface. In our lives, we can have a breakdown since we have given things a chance to develop for so long. We let the blame or the distress devour us, and we have disregarded God. Be that as it may, He is sufficiently intense to evacuate the development.

As we clean, we as a rule have a material or gloves to shield our skin from getting the cleaning arrangement specifically on us and to keep the earth off us. This insurance is expected to shield us from germs and chemicals. God's insurance for us is vastly improved than material or gloves. He gives us defensive layer as assurance from the foe. Similarly, as the things we clean need security, so do our hearts and psyches.

Keeping our homes clean takes a considerable measure of work. It is difficult, and the time has come expending, however, it is profitable to have a perfect home. Our hearts and brains require persistent reestablishment with God to remain clean. We must be mindful so as not to give the layers a chance to begin to develop again on the grounds that it can turn out to be additional tedious to start the procedure once more.

Normal profound upkeep keeps us purified every day. Standard profound help kept us far from diversions and concentrated on what we have to improve the situation God. Normal otherworldly help enables God to work through us. Every day, He helps us day by day to remember how messy we got the day preceding. He demonstrates to us what we can do to enhance with the goal that our development will never surpass us again. He scrubs us day by day, so He can have any kind of effect through us.

Need more inspiration? It would be ideal if you visit [http://www.a-plusconsulting.net] and agree to accept our free day by day quiet times with respect to how you can apply God's assertion to your life.

Weekly

It is critical to keep an agenda of errands that should be finished all the time. Certain parts of your home should be cleaned week by week, and others should be cleaned month to month or yearly.

We live quick paced lives and in some cases disregard, overlook or essentially don't know that there are things that should be cleaned on a week after week premise. To enable you to increase promote learning of week after week cleaning tasks, I have accumulated a rundown with a few hints to help you on your way with week after week cleaning.

Cleaning the various kinds of Furniture should never be an uphill task; you can easily get it done even without moving them out of your living room. Upholstered furniture can be gotten without removing it from the room. To do this, take a clammy fabric (old sheet) to cover furniture and remove fine tidy with a specific stick. To clear lacquered and cleaned furniture, heat up a glass of lager with a bit of wax. Apply somewhat warm mass to the furniture and let it dry, and after that rub with a woolen material. You can utilize vegetable oil too.

Water rings on the varnished surface are to be sprinkled with flour and afterward take a cushion absorbed the plant or motor oil, and rub until the point when it vanishes.

Mahogany furniture is wiped with the soggy material, and afterward with a dry cloth texture.

Cleaning windows and entryways should be just as easy as the rest of the house. Entryways and window edges ought to be washed with water and smelling salts (1 tablespoon fluid alkali for each 1 liter of water). Entryways, casings, and hued paint, ought to be evacuated with warm stressed tea imbue (2 teaspoons of dry tea per 1 liter of high temp water). Stains on the glass from the dry white can be deleted with the assistance of a wellbeing disposable cutter; the remains of crisp paint are expelled with turpentine. Clothes for washing windows ought to be material, or you can just utilize daily paper, which won't streak.

Cleaning mirrors is one of the super fun chores as you get to admire your beautiful self. Mirrors are to be cleaned with a cotton cushion soaked with denatured liquor and afterward dried with delicate paper or daily paper. Vigorously debased mirrors can be washed with the accompanying piece: 2 mugs high temp water, 50 g of vinegar and 50 g of chalk, blend well and let settle. Once the fluid is settled, wipe a mirror with it, and after that wipe it clean with a delicate material or daily paper

Cleaning floors is considered to be quite an uphill task; this shouldn't be the case though. It is not prescribed to wash parquet floors habitually. With cautious dealing with, parquet might be cleaned close to twice every year. To make tile floors sparkle, make use of equal amounts of wax and turpentine. Stains on a tile floor can be expelled with emery paper, and wiped with the old oil. On the off chance that the stain remains, sprinkle it with powder, cover with blotching paper and iron it. Ink stains from flooring can be expelled with emery paper or pumice too.

It is also of prime importance for you to watch over the floor coverings. Twice every year, you can clean the cover with a hairbrush, dampened with water and alkali (2 tablespoons of liquor for each 1 liter of water). In the wake of cleaning the cover in this way, it ought to be dried with a perfect material.

Expelling stains from cover:

Lager, wine, or alcohol can be pulled back from the cover with the assistance of warm water blended with powdered clothing cleanser.

Espresso and cocoa can be washed off with frosty water and glycerol (1 tablespoon for every 1 liter of water). Red wine and organic product juice stains can be expelled with the assistance of frosty water and a little measure of smelling salts. Bear in mind: once the stain is evacuated, the whole cover must be wiped with material brushes, saturated with a cleanser arrangement, at that point normally dried with a wipe.

CONCLUSION

Life isn't meant to be complicated and stressful. We make it that way with what we choose to do with our lives. So, by realizing that your life doesn't have to be complicated, you're ready to pursue a simple and enjoyable life!

Now that you're on your way to finding out how a simple life can benefit your way of thinking and how you live your life, you can begin to enjoy your simple life. Since you're so used to making decisions based on a busy and full life, having time to enjoy the simple things in life might be a new concept to you. What would you do if you could take a breath and enjoy life for what it is?

If you haven't thought about pursuing a simpler lifestyle, then I encourage you to give it a try. There are many people I know of who are taking the next steps to getting rid of the excess in their lives, and I can already see a difference in their lives. They just seem happier and more fulfilled.

Take the chance at being happy. Declutter and see how it can benefit you. I'm living a simple lifestyle and loving it, and I'm sure you will too if you will give it a chance. Good luck!

P.S. I would be very grateful if you leave your feedback on the book, tell us what exactly helped you, share your story and thus help other people find the necessary information and support. Write a customer review

Sincerely, Darlene Tucker

YOUR FREE GIFT

I wanted to show my appreciation that you support my work

so I've put together a free gift for you.

<u>My check list:</u>
«<u>Cleaning schedule</u>»

Just visit the link above to download it now.

I know you will love this gift.

Thanks!